Hear His Voice
Be His Voice

Dr. Ray L. Self

CONTENTS

I dedicate this book to people who know in their hearts that God has been speaking to them but struggle with doubts. For those who have been ridiculed because you told someone that God was talking to you, I understand.

Special thanks to my wife, Christie, who encouraged me to continue to write and finish this project.

FORWARD

It has been on my heart to write this book for a long time. I fully realize there are numerous books about the gift of prophecy, but I hope this book will be a little different and more comfortable to utilize. I feel that many believers today view God as an unapproachable supernatural being in the sky. God is the untouchable creator of the universe. Despite our view of God as the big guy in heaven who cannot be approached by mere humans, He wants to talk to us. He wants to interact with us as our Father, who converses with His children. That is the plain and simple truth.

Years ago, I was in a store and overheard two clerks having a conversation. It went something like this, "Hey man, can you believe this? I have a friend who thinks God speaks to her. She said that she could hear Him. Is this girl crazy or what?" That conversation saddened me. That God is real and alive to me is an understatement. He speaks to me. He speaks to you. Though you may not recognize His voice, this is undeniably the truth. God speaks to His creation, especially His children.

In the conservative Baptist church I attended as a child, we learned about God primarily in Sunday school class. I heard stories about God and the various characters in the Bible. The stories were quite exciting and greatly influenced my life. My problem was the God of these stories became just another storybook character. God was the central character in the book called the Bible. I read that He was the one who created the earth. He was the one who parted the Red Sea. He was the one who saved Daniel from the mouth of the lion and the one who gave David the strength to slay Goliath. God became a character in many old stories I was expected to know. He was loftily set away from a kid named Ray. I could imagine Him. I could see Him sitting on His big throne in Heaven, surrounded by angels with streets of gold. I believed in God, but He was very distant from me.

I had a moment that changed everything

This concept of God is universal. He is the big guy in Heaven who is in charge. He is the creator of the universe and someone you don't want to cross. Much of my life, this was my view of God. It is also the view of many people today.

I had a moment in my life that changed everything. Everything I valued was coming apart; I was depressed and lost. My marriage was in trouble, and my finances were coming undone. My children were having problems. I had searched for happiness with money and success. Now it seemed, I was going to lose it all.

Around that time, as a businessman, I was traveling down a two-lane highway in North Mississippi. I have no recollection of what I was thinking at the time, but I know I wasn't thinking about the Lord. At that stage of my life, most of my thoughts were about my failing marriage and my financial troubles. As I was driving my pickup truck down the road, I suddenly heard a voice. The voice said, "Ray, I have called you into the ministry." I was in the truck alone, but that voice sounded like someone speaking to me from the passenger seat. Frightened, I jerked the steering wheel and ran partially off the road. There was nothing I could do. I knew what I had heard. Was the voice audible, or was it in my head? I do not know. It was clear, and I still remember it today, although it happened over 30 years ago.

I knew that God had spoken to me. I cannot tell you how I knew, but I knew. Working in the ministry was not part of my plan. I had no thoughts of being a minister. I planned to be successful in business and make a lot of money, have plenty of fun, and enjoy life. I didn't know what to think about my marriage, but the thought trapped me that material objects would somehow bring me happiness.

God spoke to me. This God, of whom I had read and still perceived as distant and unapproachable, talked to me. He spoke to me, and I could not deny it. With no idea what to do next, I just kept doing what I was doing.

> **God spoke to me.**

A short time later, while on a family vacation to a beautiful and relaxing beach, I was sitting on a large piece of driftwood when I heard that voice speak again. This time the voice said, "Ray, I want you to stay close to me." That was all I heard, but it seemed to me that it was probably a warning. Boy, oh, boy! I was right!

My life started to unravel. Over the next several years, I had a severe business failure, complications with the IRS, and more difficulties with my marriage. Things collapsed around me. I began to understand why God said to stay close to Him. I needed Him more than ever.

Things were not fantastic, but I can tell you that I became closer to God. In response to His calling, I enrolled in Bible College. Upon finishing, I preached at various churches and completed a doctorate. After graduating, I became the president of the Bible College, where I earned my degree. It was during this time, in 1986, I received the baptism of the Holy Spirit. This fantastic event changed my life. It was the turning point in my relationship with God. He came upon me and empowered me with His Holy Spirit and transformed me from the inside out. My life changed dramatically. There were difficult times ahead, but because the Holy Spirit had renewed me, I did more than just survive; I began to thrive!

This book is not about my story. This book is about God's voice and how God speaks to His children. Sadly, His children are not listening. I have learned that we can train our ears to hear God. There is nothing more important than hearing what God has to say. His voice is vital for your welfare, family, and marriage. Your church and your community need to hear from God. God wants us to listen to Him. He wants to use us as His spokespersons.

As a parent, do you not speak to your children? Do you not expect your children to recognize your voice? Do you not expect your children to hear your voice and do what you say? How much better a parent is God, who created all of us? How much more does God want us to hear, obey Him, and respond to His voice? A believer can be trained to recognize the voice of God.

This book is logical, practical, and based on Scripture. I discuss the gifts of the Holy Spirit, specifically, prophecy. Some teach that spiritual gifts, like prophecy, were only for Bible times, but that is not what the Bible says. Sadly, some denominations teach this fallacy. People can take scriptures out of context to make the Bible say whatever they want. I have no intention of getting into a theological debate on this point. The gift of prophecy is genuinely God speaking. When God speaks a message that is for another person, and we repeat that message to them, we have given a prophecy. It is that simple.

The Word teaches us that all believers are to desire to prophesy. All children of God can hear His voice and speak for Him.

"Pursue love, yet desire earnestly spiritual gifts, but especially that you may prophesy." (1 Cor 14:1).

When I speak what I believe God has said to me, I am a spokesperson for God. I am not God. I am just delivering a message.

Before proceeding, I want to address a grave issue that has caused division within the church. When one says they hear God speak or God talks to them, some will immediately ridicule it because we have the written word of God. Many say the Bible is the only way God speaks to us. To say that the Bible is the

final spoken words of God is to ignore what the Bible says. Throughout the Bible, we have countless examples of God speaking to His people. God spoke to Abraham. God spoke to Jacob and Moses. He spoke to Daniel. The Lord spoke to Jeremiah. God spoke to Isaiah and David. He spoke to Mary and Joseph. The list goes on and on and on.

New Testament scripture declares that God speaks to us. It does not state that God stopped talking to us. Jesus made this point very clear: *"My sheep hear My voice, and I know them, and they follow Me."* (John 10:27). Jesus was speaking symbolically. He is the shepherd, and we are His sheep. Logically, if we are Christians and followers of Christ, He is speaking to us. An indication that we are Christians is we hear His voice. Jesus never said we would only hear His voice through scriptures. He was speaking to the people who were

following Him before the writing of the New Testament. In other words, Jesus speaks to us. He wants us to hear His voice and follow His instructions. Many Christians will tell you they believe beyond any doubt the Bible is the word of God, but then stumble in obeying what scripture says.

We have a powerful example of God speaking directly to His children with the story of Saul (later to become Paul) when he traveled to Damascus. *"As he was traveling, it happened that he was approaching Damascus, and suddenly a light from heaven flashed around him; and he fell to the ground and heard a voice saying to him, "Saul, Saul, why are you persecuting Me?" And he said, "Who are You, Lord?" And He said, "I am Jesus whom you are persecuting,* but *get up and enter the city, and it will be told you what you must do."* (Acts 9:4). Saul heard a voice. Was it audible? Yes, of course, because those with him heard it as well. (Acts 9:7) *The men who traveled with him stood speechless, hearing the voice but seeing no one."* (Acts 9:3-6).

The Bible is our instruction book. It teaches us that God speaks. The Bible did not say that God quit talking to His children several thousand years ago. God has been speaking throughout the history of humanity. It is senseless to say God stopped speaking when the printing of the Bible, though that is precisely what many denominations teach.

I hear messages from God when I read the Bible, yet I know beyond any shadow of a doubt that God has spoken to my heart, mind, and spirit. Millions of Christians testify to having heard from our Lord. Our heavenly Father is alive and wants a relationship with us. Those who teach that He does not speak except through the Bible are sadly mistaken. The Bible is the word of God. I believe it with all my heart. It is a sacred book that teaches us God wants to interact with His people. There are numerous examples of Him interacting in this manner. I know that God still speaks to His children today, not only through His written word but through His beautiful voice.

> I know God still speaks today.

CHAPTER 1, GOD'S USER MANUAL

"Do you believe the Bible is the word of God?" I pose this question to Christians in various group settings. Every time, the response is an escalating, "Yes." "Is the Bible true?" Again, the answer is affirmative. "So logically, if the Bible is the word of God and the Bible is true, then we should do what it says." The overwhelming response is the same – "Yes!" the audience not realizing it is a trick question.

Few Christians find difficulty obeying the commandments *"Love your neighbor as yourself,"* (*New American Standard*, Mark 12: 31 or Matthew 22:39) or *"Love God with all your heart and all your might,"* (Luke 10:27). Most biblical commandments require a response. When the Bible gives us a command, we can respond in one of four ways: 1) We can refuse to follow the commandment. 2) We can ignore the commandment. 3) We can halfheartedly attempt to obey the commandment. 4) We can obey the commandment with faith and corresponding action. Three of these responses do not please God. The best answer is to follow the commandment with your faith and action.

> **We can respond to the Bible in three ways.**

As Christians, we have a challenge given to us in many scriptures -

"Pursue love, yet desire earnestly spiritual gifts, but especially that you may prophesy." (1 Cor 14:1).
"For you can all prophesy one by one so that all may learn and all may be exhorted;" (1 Cor 14:31).
"Therefore, my brethren, desire earnestly to prophesy, and do not forbid to speak in tongues." (1 Cor 14:39).

"Truly, truly, I say to you, he who believes in Me, the works that I do, he will do also; and greater works than these he will do; because I go to the Father." (John 14:12)

What is our response to these Scriptures? We know the Bible is true. It is the word of God, and we should obey God, but are we? Why would God ask us to do something that we could not do? It does not sound fair. A loving Father would not tell His children they were capable of this if they were not able. Would you ask your children to do something they are incapable of doing?

Many people make scripture fit personal preconceptions because of previous beliefs or teaching. How do I make the Bible agree with me? I can take verses out of context to justify my formally held conviction. Because I have never experienced a specific concept, I may ignore other verses. Unfortunately, historically, many denominations base their theology on scriptures taken out of context.

I think the most important thing we, as believers, can do is to allow the Bible to speak for itself. That sounds like something straightforward to do, but we tend to read the Bible through filters based on past personal history or previous teachings. Sometimes, the interpretation comes from a lack of experience.

Let the Bible speak for Itself.

The key to understanding the Bible is to pay close attention to clear scriptures. A clear scripture in context always outweighs vague scriptures. In other words, the clear scripture interprets the obscure. Unfortunately, people interpret scriptures to support previous erroneous teaching. This method is only possible by using scripture out of context. The general rule of interpreting scripture is this; the literal sense of every text is to be taken if it is not contrary to some other texts. In that case, the obscure text is to be interpreted by those that speak more plainly.

We need to focus on clear scriptures within the context of God's Word. The Bible has many scriptures about spiritual gifts. Specifically, the gift of prophecy used to convey God speaking to us. The Bible teaches, "*My sheep hear my voice, and I know them, and they follow Me.*" (John 10:27). Hearing God speak is critical if we are to follow Him and be His witness. The Bible is also clear we are to be ambassadors of Christ, to be His voice to the church and the world.

The Scriptures used by some groups to suggest the supernatural gifts of the Holy Spirit have become obsolete, are vague and out of context. God has spoken throughout the history of man. Numerous scriptures indicate God spoke directly to man. It is unimaginable that suddenly, in modern times, God has decided to stop talking to us. Some denominations doggedly cling to their belief God only speaks to us through the written word. (The doctrine of the Church of Christ is one example of this). The Bible contradicts this doctrine.

God spoke audibly many times to His people, and it was not written until later.

God spoke to Adam "*Then the LORD God said, "It is not good for the man to be alone; I will make him a helper suitable for him."* (Gen 2:18).

God spoke to Moses, "*When the LORD saw that he turned aside to look, God called to him from the midst of the bush and said, "Moses, Moses!" And he said, "Here I am."* (Exo 3:4).

God spoke in a voice to the prophet Joel *"The word of the LORD that came to Joel, the son of Pethuel:"* (Joel 1:1), to warn God's people about an invasion of locust.

God spoke to Jeremiah *"Now the word of the LORD came to me saying, 'Before I formed you in the womb I knew you, And before you were born I consecrated you; I have appointed you a prophet to the nations.'"* (Jer 1:4-5).

God spoke to Hosea, *"When the LORD first spoke through Hosea, the LORD said to Hosea…."* (Hos 1:2).

God spoke to Joshua, *"Now it came about after the death of Moses the servant of the LORD, that the LORD spoke to Joshua, the son of Nun, Moses' servant, saying…."* (Jos 1:1).

God spoke to Jesus, *"Do you not believe that I am in the Father, and the Father is in Me? The words that I say to you I do not speak on My own initiative, but the Father abiding in Me does His works."* (John 14:10).

God spoke to Paul, *"and he fell to the ground and heard a voice saying to him, "Saul, Saul, why are you persecuting Me?" And he said, "Who are You, Lord?" And He said, "I am Jesus whom you are persecuting."* (Acts 9:4-5)

It is safe to say, as a Christian, the Bible is my user manual. The Bible is my guidebook for life. It carries instructions, encouragement, answers, and wisdom to address every problem. The Bible has proven

The Bible has proven itself.

itself historically, scientifically, logically, and supernaturally. The Bible is the truth and the word of God. We are called to be obedient to the word of God.

My observation is Christians tend to be selective with Scriptures they will obey. They tend to pick out favorite Scriptures and say, "we are standing on the word." The problem is that many times it is a verse taken out of context. It is possible to make the Bible comply with a preconception by using verses out of context.

"Each one must do just as he has purposed in his heart, not grudgingly or under compulsion, for God loves a cheerful giver." (2 Cor 9:7).

This verse is not difficult to follow. It tells us to give what feels right in your heart. "Okay, I can do that" — this what many Christians do with the easy parts of the Bible. But when we come to Scriptures that require supernatural faith, we stumble over them and sometimes ignore them. Disregarding the Scripture does not negate it. The Word is still sovereign, and God expects us to obey.

Consider this verse – *Pursue love, yet desire earnestly spiritual gifts, but especially that you may prophesy.* (1 Cor 14:1). Chase love! It is the main thing. God is love. Love should be our motivation. If our motivation is something other than love, God is not motivating us. The second commandment in this Scripture is to desire spiritual gifts. To desire spiritual gifts is not a suggestion or something that God said is optional. He said very plainly to desire spiritual gifts earnestly.

God wants us to desire spiritual gifts. The reason for this command is answered in this verse: *"But to each one is given the manifestation of the Spirit for the common good."* (1 Cor 12:7). Spiritual gifts are intended to benefit everyone. God is concerned with all

His children. Therefore, He wants us all to desire spiritual gifts. In our church culture, we expect our church leaders to have spiritual gifts, but the congregation is only to watch the show.

God gave the commandment; to desire spiritual gifts. But the last part of the Scriptures speaks another commandment. It is to especially desire the gift of prophecy. Why would God ask us to desire something that is not available? Would you ask your children to do something impossible for them? Is not God, our Father, the most loving parent we could ever imagine? If God asks us to do something, then we are capable of doing it, and we can possess it.

God asked us to desire to prophesy. When we look at Scripture we see example after example, that prophecy was God speaking, whether to an individual, community, group, or a nation. It is God's voice. Practically speaking, prophecy means to speak for another. In the Bible, when a prophet spoke, he was speaking for God. He was delivering a message from the Lord. To prophesy is to hear God's voice and be God's voice. It is a commandment for all of us. Though we try to ignore or disregard it, we cannot change the truth. The order is there. As soldiers of Christ, we are called to obey.

I believe with all my heart that every believer can hear God's voice and obey Him in regards to other people, our family, and whatever community God sends us to serve. The traditional church I attended as a child did not teach this, but that does not change what the word of God says. This commandment is for all believers. It is clear, and it calls for a response.

I have known many individuals who say, "I cannot do it, that is not who I am." We go back to the problem. Why would God ask you to prophesy if you cannot do it? Having been taught only parts of the Bible my entire life, my belief is we should look at the whole Word of God, indiscriminately, and not only what is easy or convenient. Why is this so important? God wants to be heard and obeyed, as well as worshipped and loved.

John Wesley once said that men tend to build their theology based on their lack of experience. It is interesting if we do not believe something to be true for today or have not had an encounter with it, we can take scriptures out of context to support our preconceptions. This tendency is very natural.

Sadly, we hear some ridiculous points proclaimed from the pulpit based on scriptures out of context. One of the worst was from a famous prosperity preacher using scripture to support his view of wealth - *But the manifestation of the Spirit is given to every man to profit withal.* (King James Version, 1 Cor 12:7). I was in the audience and heard him say – "This verse says that the Holy Spirit is given to help us make a profit." Ugh!

> Many people take scripture out of context to support their preconceptions.

By taking scriptures out of context, we can argue that ALL the gifts of the Spirit have passed away, but it is not what the Bible says. The Bible repeatedly says we all need to hear God's voice. The Bible shouts to us to listen to God, hear God, and obey God. We are commanded to operate in spiritual gifts.

The Bible shows us by the example of Christ to be a witness for Him by doing His same works. *"Truly, truly, I say to you, he who believes in Me, the works that I do, he will do also; and greater works than these he will do; because I go to the Father."* (John 14:12). I believed Jesus did miracles because He was the Son of God, not something within the abilities of mere mortals. It was not until later I began to realize we were supposed to do wonders, as well. Throughout Scripture, there are examples of believers flowing in the supernatural; Jesus commanded us to operate in the supernatural, too. Jesus was our teacher. He was, also, our example to follow. He made it clear, as believers, we are to follow His model.

A shepherd is not like a cowboy. A cowboy herds cows in the direction he wants them to go by getting behind them and making a lot of noise. A shepherd leads by speaking calmly and walking in front of the flock of sheep. They know his voice and follow him as he leads. How will we ever follow Jesus if we do not recognize His voice? Prophecy is the voice of God. The Lord wants all believers to know His voice. If we are a witness of Christ, we are called to be His voice by His example, with word and deed in the world today.

The Bible is a supernatural book. It is our instruction manual, not just an interesting collection of stories. We are to read the Bible as a manual to teach us how to live. Bible stories give us many examples of God's power flowing through believers.

> *"…and my message and my preaching were not in persuasive words of wisdom, but in demonstration of the Spirit and of power, so that your faith would not rest on the wisdom of men but on the power of God. (1 Cor 2:4-5).*

Paul, the Apostle, told us his words were not where people should rest their faith. He said to those reading and listening to his letters, their faith should rest on the power of God working through him. If we are obedient to God and His word, should we not also allow the power of God to work through us? We should not only tell people about Jesus but show people the power of God working through us by the Holy Spirit.

Most people feel utterly unworthy and unqualified to do this. Paul felt the same way as shown in this verse, *"I was with you in weakness and in fear and in much trembling,"* (1 Cor 2:3). Indeed, this is overwhelming and seems impossible, but we serve a supernatural God. If we could do this through natural ability, then all credit would go to us, instead of glorifying God.

There is a vast difference between a storybook and a user manual. A storybook is entertaining and informative, as it tells us stories of what happened long ago. A user manual instructs us how we are to live and act today. Our biblical user manual contains many stories to give us examples and lessons to assist in our learning. You can choose to read the Bible as a fascinating book of stories or read the Bible as instructions from our Lord and Savior with the purpose of obedience.

As a young Christian growing up in a traditional church, I was taught many stories of the Bible. Looking back, however, I was not informed about certain sections of the Bible. In my early education, for some reason, many passages were omitted. I thought I was learning the whole Bible, but honestly, I was learning only the parts of the Bible my traditional church favored, with parts of the Scripture being left out.

> As a youth I was not taught about the baptism of the Holy Spirit.

I did not learn about the baptism of the Holy Spirit. I did not learn about prophecy, words of knowledge, words of wisdom, the gift of discernment, tongues, and interpretation of tongues, as gifts for the body of Christ. I was not taught against those things - I was just never informed about them. My education was correct on the subjects that were covered. However, the information left out was a severe mistake. As Christians, we should always follow the Word, as the full counsel of God, not just our favorite verses. That is the only way we will gain a thorough understanding of the beautiful message of the Bible.

CHAPTER 2, I ENCOUNTER THE HOLY SPIRIT

In my early church days, I was not taught much about the Holy Spirit. That does not change the fact the Holy Spirit is real, and he is a person, and he is a part of the Trinity, and he is mentioned throughout Scripture. I think the church concentrated on favorite passages of Scripture that were in alignment with their previously held beliefs. Teachers tend to pass on whatever they were previously taught. Therefore, it is easy for omissions to be passed on from generation to generation.

Jesus spoke of the importance of the Holy Spirit *"But I tell you the truth, it is to your advantage that I go away; for if I do not go away, the Helper will not come to you; but if I go, I will send Him to you.* (John 16:7). This verse is one of those fantastic verses that I call real "mind blowers." Imagine you are a disciple over 2000 years ago walking with Jesus. You have had the incredible experience of watching the Son of God perform miracles, raise the dead, heal the sick, and cast out demons. You had the privilege of actually walking with Him, spending time with Him, and face-to-face being His friend. Imagine being in ministry with the Son of God in the flesh. What could get any better than that? But then Jesus said to the same disciples that they would be better off if He leaves. I can only imagine their first thoughts, "What! Are you kidding me? That's crazy. No Way!"

> **Understand the importance of having the Holy Spirit live within you.**

But Jesus was trying to get them to understand the importance of having the Spirit of God come and be with them and live within them for the rest of their life. Jesus made it clear that when He ascended into heaven, He was going to send the Holy Spirit to be in us. In actuality, Jesus was saying it is better to have God living in you and being with you all the time than walking with Him during His life on earth.

Now, as Christians, we have the same opportunity to have the Holy Spirit, the Spirit of God living inside of us. The Spirit of God is essential to understand because it is the Holy Spirit who gives us the power and the ability to hear God's voice, be God's voice, and perform the Lord's ministry.

"but you will receive power when the Holy Spirit has come upon you; and you shall be My witnesses both in Jerusalem, and in all Judea and Samaria, and even to the remotest part of the earth. (Acts 1:8).

The promise is clear that when the Holy Spirit comes upon us, we will receive power and the ability to be witnesses for Christ.

I will share a story with you. Years ago, in the mid-eighties, my life was a mess. When I say a mess, it is an understatement. I had been a successful businessman, but everything crashed and burned. I had multiple problems hitting me on every side of my life. I was suffering from depression. I lived in constant frustration, fear, stress, and hopelessness. I am not going into all the details of everything that had happened to me. Some of it was my fault, and much of it not my fault. It was an extremely dark period in my life.

My mother and I would talk and pray on the phone quite a bit. One day she shared with me that she had a friend from church named John, who prayed for people in his home. My mother told me a friend of hers from church shared that she could not have a child. John prayed for her, and now she has a baby. My mother shared that John often prayed for people in his home, and many miracles had taken place there. Something in me immediately decided to meet this man. My mother made arrangements and took me to his home. John was an accomplished painter who lived in an elegant house in a beautiful neighborhood in Memphis, Tennessee.

I noticed upon walking into his home the exquisite landscape paintings hanging in his living room. He shared that those were his originals and that he had paintings on display in galleries in New York City and other major cities around this country. I love beautiful paintings. John impressed me with his very humble attitude.

Then John said something interesting to me. He said, "Ray, have you ever heard of the baptism of the Holy Spirit?" I replied, "no." I was not quite sure what he was referencing. John kindly said he wanted to share some Scriptures with me, and I said, "okay." The first verse John shared with me was *"for John baptized with water, but you will be baptized with the Holy Spirit not many days from now."* (Acts 1:5). Then John shared this verse with me *"but you will receive power when the Holy Spirit has come upon you; and you shall be My witnesses both in Jerusalem, and in all Judea and Samaria, and even to the remotest part of the earth.* (Acts 1:8).

John had my full attention; he very politely shared more Scripture with me. He was like an attorney building his case but doing it in a very loving and humble manner. Next, he shared the story of Philip:

> *"Philip went down to the city of Samaria and began proclaiming Christ to them. The crowds with one accord were giving attention to what was said by Philip, as they heard and saw the signs which he was performing.* (Acts 8:5 – 6).

"But when they believed Philip preaching the good news about the kingdom of God and the name of Jesus Christ, they were being baptized, men and women alike." (Acts 8:12).

"Now when the apostles in Jerusalem heard that Samaria had received the word of God, they sent them Peter and John, who came down and prayed for them that they might receive the Holy Spirit. For He had not yet fallen upon any of them; they had simply been baptized in the name of the Lord Jesus. Then they began laying their hands on them, and they were receiving the Holy Spirit." (Act 8:14 – 17).

This story impacted me. I saw something in Scripture I had not seen before. When Philip preached the gospel, people were being saved and baptized. I was very familiar with that principle because my church preached the gospel. People got saved and baptized regularly, including me. What I saw in Scripture was two different things happening. I read people were believing, being saved and baptized through Philips preaching, which made perfect sense to me. Later, the apostles came up and prayed for them to receive the Holy Spirit. That is two separate events! I thought to myself, "Why wasn't I told about this? There is something after salvation that I desperately need!" The Bible says I shall receive power, and when the Holy Spirit comes upon me. I knew my life in crisis was indeed in need of the power of God. I needed something greater than myself. I needed God to do something, and I needed a change, and I knew it would take a power greater than me to cause this change!

> **There was something after salvation that I needed.**

But my new friend John was not done yet. He proceeded to show me in another example from Scripture:

"It happened that while Apollos was at Corinth, Paul passed through the upper country and came to Ephesus, and found some disciples. He said to them, "Did you receive the Holy Spirit when you believed?" And they said to him, "No, we have not even heard whether there is a Holy Spirit." And he said, "Into what then were you baptized?" And they said, "Into John's baptism." Paul said, "John baptized with the baptism of repentance, telling the people to believe in Him who was coming after him, that is, in Jesus." When they heard this, they were baptized in the name of the Lord Jesus. And when Paul had laid his hands upon them, the Holy Spirit came on them, and they began speaking with tongues and prophesying." (Acts 19:16).

In this story, Paul met believers who were baptized but had not yet received the power of the Holy Spirit. When Paul laid hands on them, they received this power. It was apparent to me from Scripture, there is a baptism of the Holy Spirit. It is a separate event from salvation. In my heart I knew this was the missing piece in my life.

The next occurrence was a pivotal point in my life. John put his hand on my shoulder and began to pray. I do not remember the exact words, but it was something like, "I baptize Ray, my brother with the Holy Spirit. I ask you to come upon him now."

All of a sudden, I began to feel things I have never felt before. The first thing I remember was feeling warmth flowing from the top of my head down over my body. It was a very peaceful, warm sensation that began to spill all over me. At that time in my life, I was completely stressed, fearful, anxious, and depressed. To feel any peace was terrific. This warmth was something I had never felt before. The peaceful feeling was completely overwhelming me. I then realized I felt a sense of love. It was a love I had never felt before. It was a saturating love that made me feel wholly accepted and loved unconditionally. It was an incredible feeling to have peace and love during a horrible dark and scary storm. My life was like living in the middle of a tornado with problems swirling all around me. All I could see was darkness, but now I felt peace and love. Wow! Then I had another sensation. I felt a strange surge of power come over me. I knew whatever was happening to me was huge. The power that came over me is difficult to describe, but it came after the sense of peace and love. The whole experience gave me a fantastic sense of the power of the Holy Spirit. I did not feel personally powerful, but there was power around me, and something powerful had come upon me for sure.

I must have sat there for quite a long time because at some point I heard my mother say, "Ray, are you okay? Ray, Ray." I remember thinking everyone needs to be still and be quiet. I was experiencing something beautiful and did not want it to end. Excuse the figure of speech. But I was in heaven. After some time, I opened my eyes and felt terrific.

John began to give me instructions. I felt so peaceful; I was willing to hear anything he said. John said from now on, whenever I read Scripture, I will see and understand things in the Bible I have never seen or understood before. (I thought that was very interesting).

He said when I pray for people, I should expect every one of them to be healed. He suggested that I go to a particular church that understood the Holy Spirit and could help me. He also asked me an odd question. John said, "Ray, do you have any strange words that seem to be forming in your mouth?" I said, "No. Not that I know of." I thought to myself, that was a strange question. Then John said to me, "if you feel words are forming in your mind, it may sound like gibberish, but it is not. It will be the gift of tongues. Do not let the Devil convince you that that is gibberish."

When the evening came to a close, I drove home. My mother and I were in separate cars. As I was driving, I began to hear a very strange phrase in my mind; one I will never forget. It was like the words were forming in my mouth. It was a phrase of an unknown language. I began to speak it over and over again. Now you can believe what you want, but I received a gift of tongues and started with just a few words, but my prayer language began to grow and has continued to grow since then.

It was a phrase of an unknown language.

I was baptized with the Holy Spirit, and my life was never the same. I do not know why the baptism of the Holy Spirit is so controversial because the Scriptures are very plain concerning it. Again, like John Wesley, I think people still tend to build their theology on their lack of experience or traditional doctrine instead of this letting the Bible speak for itself. It is critical if we are to hear God, obey God, and be His witness. We have the power of God flowing through us. Salvation is the first and most crucial step. Without salvation, there is no hope. After salvation, we need the power of God to be an effective witness for Jesus Christ. It is so essential that Jesus instructed His disciples to wait in Jerusalem until they received the power from on high. (Luke 24:49) He did not want them to begin witnessing for Him until they received the power to do it. The same applies to us today. If we are to be an effective witness for Christ, do what God has created and called us to do, we must have the power of the Holy Spirit, flowing through us. Jesus was trying to show and teach us throughout His ministry, we need the supernatural power of God. He told us if you have the Holy Spirit in you, then you can do the same things that He did, but wait till you have power before you try to do it (Luke 24:49). That is the message of the gospel for us. We need to hear His voice and be His voice. To do that, we must have the power of the Holy Spirit with us. Listening to His voice and obeying what His voice is telling us to do, it is critical. I encourage you to not close your mind to this. Read the Bible for yourself and study it. Do not let the traditions of man override what the Bible says plainly.

We need the power of God living with and in us. God communicates to us through the Holy Spirit dwelling in us. We cannot follow Jesus without hearing His voice. I do not believe you can effectively hear His voice without the baptism of the Holy Spirit. How can we be a witness for Christ if we cannot hear his voice? Jesus spoke about this very clearly in one of His parables. How can we possibly follow our shepherd, without hearing His voice? Another commandment from Scripture that we must obey. We are to listen to His voice, hear what God is telling us to do and speak what God is telling us to speak. Jesus modeled this principle very clearly *"Do you not believe that I am in the Father, and the Father is in Me? The words that I say to you I do not speak on My own initiative, but the Father abiding in Me does His works.* Jesus was saying that He was only speaking what God told Him to speak." (John 14:10). Then Jesus went on to say if you are of God, you can hear

God. *"He who is of God hears the words of God; for this reason you do not hear them, because you are not of God."* (John 8:47).

We were created to have a relationship with God. A relationship requires the ability to hear Him. He wants us to become close to Him, and that requires being able to listen to Him. It is one thing to read and study Him, which is all well and good, but it does not necessarily create a personal relationship. Just like in our everyday personal relationships, we need the art of conversation, which is the art of listening and understanding. That is what makes a quality relationship, which is one of the reasons I wrote this book. Being able to recognize God's voice and talk to Him, I believe, is the most important thing we can do. It will affect our everyday decisions and cause eternal consequences. God has given us many beautiful promises in His word. Many of those promises carry conditions such as obedience followed by action. How can I obey God if I cannot hear him?

> To be able to hear God is the most important thing we can do.

It is sad in our society that we have reduced God and Jesus to storybook characters instead of understanding they are alive, willing to dwell in us and communicate with us. This kind of relationship will compellingly change your life.

CHAPTER 3, DESIRES AND IMPLICATIONS

Desires motivate us. What we desire can determine the course of our life. Desires can be Godly or merely natural. Desires can be useful or harmful. Desires can be healthy or unhealthy. The strongest desire that has ever motivated humanity is sexual desire. We know this can be good in the context of marriage, or it can be perverted. Perverted sexual desire can lead to pornography addiction and fornication. When we want something bad enough, we will go to any extreme to have it.

The Spirit of God has a fantastic way of changing our desires. I have known Christians over the years that were afraid that God would ask them to do something they did not want to do. One friend of mine said, "I was always afraid that if I heard God speak, He would tell me He wanted me to go to Africa, and I don't want to go to Africa." It is perfectly understandable to have such concerns, but God has a wonderful answer. The Lord understands our human nature much better than we do since He created us, God in His incredible mercy does not ask us to do things without helping us to control our desires. In other words, God has an incredible influence over our desires.

> The Spirit of God has a fantastic way of changing our desires.

Consider this Scripture *"The desire of the righteous is only good, But the expectation of the wicked is wrath."* (Prov 11:23). Why are the desires of the righteous always good? Is it self discipline, or is it in their nature? The righteous have godly desires because God has instilled in them His nature. When we are "born again" of the Spirit of God, we are given a new nature, and this nature will have Godly desires.

"But I say, walk by the Spirit, and you will not carry out the desire of the flesh." (Gal 5:16). You will notice here living by the Spirit of God allows us to have Godly desires, not fleshly desires. In other words, the spirit of God in us gives us godly desires. As Christians, we choose to allow the Holy Spirit to be our influence rather than our own natural tendencies.

There is a promise in the book of Psalms, which has a condition which I believe is very simple. *"Delight yourself in the LORD; And He will give you the desires of your heart."* (Psalms 37:4). The condition of the promise is if I delight myself in the Lord, He will provide me with my desires. That verse is not saying He is going to give me my natural fleshly worldly desires. The Scripture implies that when we take joy in the relationship we have with the Lord, He will provide us with Godly desires. The principal reason is Christianity is not merely a discipline. It is a relationship. When you have a relationship with God, your desires will change.

After I received the baptism of the Holy Spirit, I found church to be incredibly fun. I could not wait to get there, and I was disappointed when the service was over. Many times, I would hang around for over an hour after the service ended. The difference between the two experiences was now I am baptized and filled with the Holy Spirit. New desires came into my heart, including the desire to worship. I had a willingness to be in His presence and hear His voice. It was nothing that I had to force or generate in my strength.

Our desires can determine the success or failure of our life. Godly desires never fail you and guarantee you God's version of peace and prosperity, which is much better than what the world offers us. It is all about the presence of God and the power of the Spirit of God filling us and living within us. The Holy Spirit changes our desires, and this transformation will change our life.

I want to share another story from my life. I was a single pastor and a single father. I had been through a painful divorce but was able to continue in ministry by the grace of God. I was a single father, working for the Lord for eight years. Honestly, I was not satisfied with being alone. I wanted to be married. I know I should say, at this point, I was content in the Lord and was happy to be single, but truly that was not the case with me. Many people have more grace for singlehood than I did. However, at that time, I was able to start multiple Bible colleges and pastor three churches. Only God can do something like this!

I decided one day after watching a TV commercial to try out the website called eHarmony. I filled out the profile and submitted it. Soon, I received a notification indicating I had several matches. The procedure is that one goes through a series of steps with these matches. You answer questions programmed to determine if this person is someone you might want to pursue a relationship. The fourth step is known as open communication. At this point, one can e-mail the person directly. If both parties are still interested, you are free to facilitate a meeting. eHarmony recommends meeting in a public place like for lunch to reduce pressure. I met several nice ladies, but nothing was working. After a while, it became overwhelming. It appeared there were many more single females on this site than males, so I became pretty popular. I decided after my unfruitful search for the perfect woman I was going to give it up. I did not think it was a tool that God intended to use. The day I had decided to cancel my membership, I received a message and a photo of a woman in Orlando, Florida, named Christie. Her picture was beautiful. She was standing on a beach by a sand dune with the wind blowing her hair and was wearing a gorgeous beach outfit. I decided perhaps I could stay with eHarmony a little longer (chuckle).

Christie and I began to e-mail back and forth. At that time, I was living in the Memphis, Tennessee, area. Our e-mails led to phone calls. I enjoyed talking to Christie. We always ended up praying together over the phone. I was very impressed with her prayer life, her heart for God, and her tender spirit. I was interested in her, but we did not know where this would lead. One day she dropped the bomb on me. She said the words no man ever wants to hear.

One day she dropped the bomb on me

In her lovely voice, she told me over the phone one day, "Ray, you are like a big brother to me." Well, that pretty much ruined any idea I had for a romantic relationship. I decided that she would be a great friend, so we continued a friendly relationship for several months only by phone conversations and e-mail.

One day I received an invitation to preach a revival in Vero Beach, Florida. My flight itinerary involved me flying from Memphis to Orlando, Florida, then driving to Vero Beach, which is several hours south. When I told Christie the news, I was pleasantly surprised when she offered to pick me up at the airport and drive me to Vero.

Christie had a ministry she called "Stories of God's Glory." She told me she would like to write my story. I felt honored and agreed. She said she would interview me and take notes and then write my story. I thanked her. Christie also said she would stay in Vero Beach, so she would have plenty of time to interview me and attend the three-night revival.

It was December 8, when I flew to Orlando to meet Christie. She had described to me exactly what she would be wearing, so I could easily recognize her at the airport. Unfortunately, she changed her mind about her clothes multiple times, ending up wearing something completely different, which I thought was hilarious. When I arrived and cleared security, I saw her holding a sign with my name on it. On the backside of the sign where only she could see, she had a picture of me. There was no way we were going to miss each other. I recognized her immediately.

We began our drive to Vero Beach and immediately got lost! This was hilarious because she is a native Floridian. We eventually made it to the hotel. After getting settled in, we met the hosting pastor for dinner. While we were at the restaurant, the pastor looked at Christie and said, "What would you say if Ray asked you to marry him?" I almost slid entirely under the table with embarrassment. Christie seemed to be surprised but said something like, well, it would have to be God's will.

> "What would you say if Ray ask you to marry him?"

I was shocked! Had the pastor heard something from God? Christie was my friend and self-proclaimed little sister! We proceeded to the church where I preached for three consecutive nights. It was there that I introduced Christie to Spirit-filled ministry. We witnessed several people miraculously healed during the services.

We stayed at the same hotel (separate rooms, of course). During the day when there was nothing to do, we went to the beach and took long walks together. We walked and talked, then went back to the hotel, where she would interview me for prolonged periods. As she interviewed me, we both felt a powerful presence of God in the room. I said, "do you feel that?" She answered, "Yes, this is amazing!" We spent long hours developing the story and chatted on the beach. I was amazed at how easy it was to talk to her and how I never got tired of it. Honestly, even with best friends, I weary of conversation after a while, but not with Christie. After the third day, we drove back to Orlando. I believe we knew something special was happening. Christie said she just felt very overwhelmed by everything. After she dropped me at the airport, she sat in her car for an hour and a half and just prayed.

I went back to Memphis and returned to my routine. As I finished teaching a class in a local church, I unmistakably heard the voice of God say to me, "Ray, Christie is my perfect gift for you." I was stunned. I knew God had spoken to me. I was astounded, nervous, excited, and did not know quite what to do. The next day, I was at the golf course, hitting practice balls. I had a serious golf addiction at that time. I am still pretty much hooked on golf. My cell phone rang, and it was Christie. I spoke to her, and I said nervously, " I am not sure if I should tell you this, but I believe God spoke to me last night." Though I felt a bit apprehensive, I just said, "Christie, I believe the Lord said, you are my perfect gift from Him." There was silence on the other end of the phone, and then I thought I heard a little gasp. Christie asked me to hold on a moment. When she returned to the phone, she said she had gone to find her journal. She then read an entry to me. The entry related to how a friend of hers had given her a prophetic word several years earlier that said, " your future husband will tell you, "God told me that you are my perfect gift from Him." It was the exact quote word for word quote God had spoken to Christie two years earlier. Though I had no knowledge of this, I had spoken the same words. I think we both nearly fainted at that moment.

> God said, "Ray, Christie is my perfect gift."

How could this possibly work? I lived and pastored a church in a small town in Mississippi just south of Memphis called Olive Branch, (cool place for a church). It was 765 miles from Orlando,

Florida. I had family and many friends in the Memphis area where I lived for the last 56 years.

I drove down to see her the day after Christmas in 2006. I was a man on a mission. Could this beautiful lady be the one? I wanted to find out. I kept thinking there is no logic to this. How could this possibly work? Amid all my mental gymnastics a Scripture came into my mind:

"For My thoughts are not your thoughts, Nor are your ways My ways," declares the LORD." (Isaiah 55:8).

The drive to Orlando was 14 hours, providing plenty of time to think. It was a strange feeling. Part of me kept saying, "Ray, what are you doing? It doesn't make sense." Another part of me could not wait to get to Orlando and to spend more time with Christie.

I arrived and spent several days with her, much of the time walking in the_park. In one park, there was a lake with a walking path around it. We walked around the lake, and it seemed that we hugged every 10 feet. After we finished the walk, we renamed the lake "Hug Lake."

We spent several beautiful days together. To my amazement, Christie told me she would like to go back with me to Memphis to meet the people at my church and my family. I was surprised but was more than pleased to do that. We ended up in Memphis for the New Year's Eve celebration. I remember we had a New Year's Eve prayer service at my church, and I was thrilled to introduce Christie to my church members. I also remember clearly at this point, I knew in my heart that she was the one. I had heard God speak, and so had Christie.

God had spoken to us at this point in three different ways. The first time was when He said to me in my mind, "Ray, Christie is my perfect gift for you." The second way He spoke was to Christie through a prophetic word given to her by a friend several years earlier. The third way He spoke was into my heart, where He gave me the peace of knowing that she was the one. There are numerous scriptural examples of this which I will not go into at this point. God speaks to us by putting words into our minds, giving us thoughts, impressions, and using other people.

After several other confirmations, Christie and I were married on the beach at Vero six months later. I can honestly say that hearing God's voice changed my life and changed the life of my wife, as well as our family and friends.

After eighteen months of having a residence in Memphis and Orlando, we decided, after much prayer and again, hearing the voice of God that we would move everything to Orlando, including my ministry. I was soon in a new town, having left behind family and friends, how could this possibly be God's will?

Once again, my future went through a dramatic change when the Lord once more spoke a vital word to me. A mutual friend of my wife introduced me to a local pastor named Joe Warner. This friend told me that Joe and I were very much alike. I tend to be a little silly and corny but also very serious about the Lord and His work. Joe Warner is famous for his puns, yet, an earnest minister. We met for lunch, and he invited me to visit his church. At that point, Christie and I had decided that we would explore the Orlando area and visit several churches to decide which one we would join. One particular Sunday, we chose to visit Freedom Fellowship Church pastored by my new friend, Joe Warner. We walked in the door, and within 30 seconds, I knew the Lord had spoken to me that this church was to be our home. I did not have the courage to tell Christie about what I had just heard. But I knew in my heart that this was where God wanted us to be.

We revisited the following Sunday, and then I experienced one of the strangest things that ever happened to me in a church service.

I was enjoying sitting near the back with my wife, not having to preach or minister but able to relax and enjoy the service. Toward the end of the service, Pastor Joe with a microphone in his hand, said, "Ray and Christie, come up front." I was thinking to myself, what could he possibly want, and why would he want us to stand in front of the church? We went up to the front, and Joe told us to turn around and face the congregation. As we did that, he announced to the church that he wanted everyone to come up and meet our two new members. I was utterly shocked!

I had not joined this church. Christie looked up at me with an expression that said, what have you done? I was clueless. We stood there in front of a long line of people that came up, shook our hands, and welcomed us as new members of Freedom Fellowship Church. On the drive home, Christie said, "Ray, did you decide to join this church and not tell me?" I said, "No." I did know the Lord had told me this is where He wanted us to be, but I had not yet shared this information with my wife. In my heart, I wanted to be sure I had heard from God. Now Joe Warner had made a public announcement that we were members of Freedom Fellowship Church! I could not understand why he did that since we never told him we wanted to join the church. We have been members of this church now for over 11 years. I laugh a lot about that day and say we never joined this church, we were drafted! Pastor Joe Warner informed me he knew this was the church where we belonged and I had told him we wanted to be members, which was not true. I believe he knew in his heart this was God's will and just took the initiative, but either way, it turned out to be one of the best decisions of our lives.

What happened in the next 11 years is a fantastic story. Because of my connection with Joe Warner and Freedom Fellowship Church, doors for ministry opened up to me all over the United States and in many foreign nations. I ended up preaching and doing conferences in places like New Orleans, Fort Lauderdale, Pittsburgh, Philadelphia, New York, Chicago, and mission trips to Guatemala, Spain, and Indonesia. I never would have imagined myself in

> I never would have imagined myself in a global ministry.

a global ministry! Indeed, God's ways are not our ways. His thoughts are not ours, as the Bible says. But for this book, I want you to understand the impact of hearing God's voice and what it can do to your life.

Through these trips, I was able to minister to thousands of people. I have seen healings, and many prophetic words come to pass. I witnessed signs, wonders, and miracles, beyond imaginings. Things I would never have experienced had I remained in my previous home. One word from God will not only change your life but can change the world around you and do things unimaginable. The president of the seminary I attended, said: "You can always tell when it's God because it's bigger than you are." This is what happens when you listen to His voice and obey, something bigger and better than you can ever imagine will always result. God knows more than you. He knows better than you. His answer is more than you could ever imagine. It is all about hearing His voice and obeying His voice.

CHAPTER 4, HIS VOICE

The story from the last chapter is to verify when God speaks, it is essential to hear and respond to Him. I pray this book will help you listen and recognize His voice, to respond to His voice, and represent Him. I pray you will become His ambassadors and be His voice in this world. Sadly, in our culture and various traditional churches, God's voice is no longer audible. You hear stories about God, such as the Christmas story or the Easter story. God is someone from the past who died thousands of years ago. In my youth, I was not taught, nor did I understand God is alive, speaking, and desiring to have a relationship with us.

I cannot overstate the importance of hearing His voice. The implications and effects on my life have been enormous. By listening to Him, thousands of people have felt the impact. What if all believers were able to hear His voice? I do not claim that anyone can listen to Him entirely. I get confused, I get distracted, and sometimes I just do not hear God speaking. I am an average person just like you. To say I sit around all day long, trying to hear God is not true, though I want to listen to him. I know listening to Him has changed my life. I believe sometimes I get lazy and too busy with everyday life. I also know that Satan has a scheme to keep us distracted and keep us away from God's voice as much as possible. He understands the threat to him when people hear and obey the voice of God. Jesus made it clear that He did not speak without first listening to His father. Jesus had the most fruitful ministry the world has ever known. His ability to hear God's voice made Jesus very successful in ministry.

"Do you not believe that I am in the Father, and the Father is in Me? The words that I say to you I do not speak on My own

initiative, but the Father abiding in Me does His works." (John 14:10).

Jesus explained in this Scripture the Holy Spirit is living inside of Him. The words He is speaking are coming from the Holy Spirit living inside Him. If you are a believer, you also have the Holy Spirit living inside of you. The Lord speaks to the Holy Spirit within you, the Holy Spirit interprets and relays the message to your mind or gives you an impression in a way you can understand. You might say the Holy Spirit is your God interpreter.

There is a principle in John (New American Standard Bible) that is critical for all believers. Look at this Scripture:

"But when He, the Spirit of truth, comes, He will guide you into all the truth; for He will not speak on His own initiative, but whatever He hears, He will speak; and He will disclose to you what is to come. "He will glorify Me, for He will take of Mine and will disclose it to you. "All things that the Father has are Mine; therefore I said that He takes of Mine and will disclose it to you." (John 16:13 – 15).

In verse 13, Jesus said the Holy Spirit would only speak to us what he has heard. In verse 14, Jesus is telling us that the Holy Spirit will always give glory to Him, receives His information, and then gives it to us. In verse 14, Jesus summarizes by telling us that what God has He gives to Jesus. Jesus gives what He has to the Holy Spirit and then the Holy Spirit gives it to us. It is a chain of command. It works like this: God gives His orders to Jesus. Jesus gives His orders to the Holy Spirit. Then the Holy Spirit relays the commands to you.

Many believers focus on learning about God and studying about Jesus, but they do not rely on the Holy Spirit living inside of them. The beautiful truth is the main characters of the Bible, God and His son are very much alive and want to have a relationship with us. The vehicle they are using is the Holy Spirit. The Holy Spirit must never be ignored or eliminated. Some Scriptures give stern warnings about this.

"do not despise prophetic utterances." (1 Thes. 5:20)

"Do not grieve the Holy Spirit of God, by whom you were sealed for the day of redemption," (Eph. 4:30).

To despise a prophetic utterance is to ignore the voice of God. The word despise is defined according to Webster - *despise, condemn, scorn, disdain, to regard as unworthy of one's notice or consideration.* According to Webster, the word *grieve* means: *to cause to suffer: distress.*

The Lord wants us to hear His voice speaking to us by the Holy Spirit. When we refuse to listen, we grieve the Holy Spirit, and we despise God's word. These are dire warnings to us. I do not believe any of us want to grieve the Holy Spirit and ignore God's voice intentionally. Honestly, this is what we tend to do.

We can offer hundreds of excuses. In our society, we can easily get caught up with our jobs and making money. Many of us are just trying to get through each day. It is a full-time occupation to be a good husband, father, wife, mother. This occupation keeps us mentally and spiritually occupied, crowding out the voice of God. It is not what we purpose to do, but our lifestyle causes us to despise the voice of God and grieve His Holy Spirit.

In my family history, there is a story about God's voice, I will never forget. When I was young, my mother suffered from what was then known as a nervous breakdown. Looking back, I believe the cause of the nervous breakdown was diet pills. In the 1950s, it was not unusual for doctors to prescribe amphetamines to help with weight loss. My mother took amphetamines as prescribed by her doctor. The effect on her mind and nervous system was terrible. She had become very depressed and was unable to take care of my two sisters and me. My father was a traveling salesman and was gone Monday through Friday every week to provide for the family. One day when my mother was in her bed, she cried out to God, "Lord, I want to die. Please let me die." Suddenly she heard a voice. She told me many times over the years that the sound was audible. The voice said, "Jamie if you're willing to die for me, will you not live for me?" My mother told me she clearly heard it. She knew God had spoken to her. He had saved her life and gave her a reason to live. Obviously, the impact upon my life was astronomical!

If you have ever suffered from depression, you know it is a very dark place. Positive thoughts just do not come. When a person is depressed, they are overwhelmed by negative thoughts and overwhelming feelings. One does not hear anything encouraging when one is depressed. My mother, at that point, was severely depressed, so depressed she wanted to die. The simple words from God gave her hope that changed her and the course of my family forever. Maybe this is why I wanted to write this book. I know when God speaks what can happen and how it can affect a life, or a future, or even thousands of people.

Suddenly she heard a voice

CHAPTER 5, CONTROL ISSUES

It is natural to desire to be in control. I believe our nature loves to have everything planned and controlled. When people think they are in control, there is a sense of security. This feeling is deceptive. We naturally have plans and ideas about the way things should happen. We have a plan for our day and a plan for our week. We have a plan for what we want to do and a plan for what we do not want to do. Unfortunately, we also have plans and ideas, how everyone else should act and what they should do. This is typical human behavior, but unfortunately, it is very unhealthy. We are comfortable when everything works out and is happening the way we think it should. It is a battle for control that everyone fights. However, much of the time the struggle is with God.

Control is a sad illusion and causes a lot of frustration, tension, and ultimately failure. Man's attempt to control was evident from the beginning, even in the Garden of Eden. Everyone knows the familiar story of Adam and Eve. God told them they should not eat of one particular tree. When Satan came into the picture and said if they do eat of that tree, they will have the same knowledge as God. So, it all began. It was not enough to be made in the image of God; they wanted to be just like God, AND BE IN CONTROL.

The first colossal lie, *"For God knows that in the day you eat from it your eyes will be opened, and you will be like God, knowing good and evil."* (Gen 3:5). They fell for it. Adam and Eve were created in God's image, but the temptation created a desire for more. The temptation offered a trade, the image of God for the same control as God. To be made in God's image should have been more than sufficient, but they were tempted with what appeared to be better.

The battle in life will always be who was in control, you or God. Our natural tendency is to want to be in charge. It makes us feel safe. It gives us a false sense of security. The problem is God, alone, is the one who is in charge. Resisting Him will lead to a life of failure and frustration.

It took me a long time to learn God knows what is best for me. If I let Him be in control, He will happily give me what is best for me. If I insist on being in charge, He will fold His hands and patiently allow me to suffer my natural consequences until once again, I reach out and let Him be in charge.

There was an old TV show called "Father Knows Best." The truth for your life is that your Father in heaven knows what is best for you. The only way to have the best is to do what Jesus did. He listened to His Father and followed His instructions. God's ideas for our lives are not our ideas; they are better. God's way is not our way. It is better.

"For My thoughts are not your thoughts, Nor are your ways My ways," declares the LORD." (Isaiah 5:8).

It feels unsettling not to be in control of ourselves. It is unnatural for us. When I know what to expect, and it plays out as I thought, there is a sense of security that comes with it. What is expected feels safe. When I make a plan, and it works the way I intended, there is an inner satisfaction. The feeling is peaceful and controlled. This is deception. Unfortunately, this desire to control can negatively affect people around us. This controlled success is not usually God's plan.

When we take control and eliminate God, we fall into traps. We may not like the way a person acts and how they make us feel; therefore, we want to control and change them. Or we may be so confident in our "rightness" that we try to convince other people they should be acting with the same "rightness" that we do. In other words, *"I know best, why don't you act the way I think you should act? Obviously, my ideas correct. Therefore, you have no excuse but to do it my way."*

The weapons of control are gruesome. They include manipulation, guilt, shame, domination, and force. When we take complete charge of our lives or try to enforce our will upon others, we are in rebellion to God. The bottom line is God is in control. That is the end of it. That is the truth. When we surrender to God's will and allow Him to be in control, wonderful things happen for us. It is a battle against our sinful nature. When we win this battle, peace, success, and contentment will be the result.

The following Scripture explains God's plan for control:

"so that the requirement of the Law might be fulfilled in us, who do not walk according to the flesh but according to the Spirit. For those who are according to the flesh set their minds on the things of the flesh, but those who are according to the Spirit, the things of the Spirit. For the mind set on the flesh is death, but the mind set on the Spirit is life and peace, because the mind set on the flesh is hostile toward God; for it does not subject itself to you will the law of God, for it is not even able to do so, and those who are in the flesh cannot please God." (Rom 8:4 -8).

When the Scripture refers to the flesh, it is referring to our natural tendencies. When the Scripture is referring to the Spirit, it is referring to God. We can set our minds on God and His ways, or we can keep our minds on ourselves, our desires, and our methods. God's requirement for us in the New Testament forbids this. The good news is: It is really for our best interest. God requires us to walk according to His Spirit. We do this by setting our mind on the Spirit and not our natural or fleshly desires. When we set our thoughts on the Holy Spirit, we are listening to the voice of God, and by doing that, we meet God's requirements. It is not an option. It is a commandment!

Our nature loves being in charge. The safe and secure feeling of being in charge is a grand deception. The security we feel is self-made. You can have false security in your ability to control your life, or you can be secure in God's ability to take charge of your life. The choice is yours. I am emphasizing this point because it is not easy or natural. We can discipline and train ourselves to be in tune with the Spirit of God and let go of personal control. We can surrender our will to His and reap His assigned harvest.

I am sure you've heard the expression, "let go and let God." This expression tells us to surrender our will to God's will. It sounds charming and effortless. The phrase is somewhat of a cliché. I think because the phrase is so common, we tend to ignore it. However, the principle of letting go and trusting God is extremely powerful. The people who struggle the most with this are those who have lived through some form of abuse.

When a person suffers the horrible experience of abuse regardless of the type, they have a feeling of being out of control. This feeling becomes embedded in the subconscious. As time passes, the feeling of being out-of-control triggers past emotions suffered during the abuse. It is feeling out-of-control that causes the old memories of abuse to resurface with the emotions attached. An abused person wants to be in control because not being in control is synonymous with past abuse. You can see how this creates a problem in our relationship with God. You can also understand why Satan loves to use this strategy against God's children.

> Abuse creates a horrible feeling of being out of control.

If you are a victim of abuse, it may be more difficult for you to surrender your will and let go of control. It is not impossible, but possibly a bit more complicated than for others. I recommend practicing letting go in small chunks. I had a pastor tell me years ago, "I have to let go every 10 minutes." Take one area of your life, one not so critical to you, and release it to God. Maybe it is a particular worry. Perhaps, it is a coworker who has intentionally offended you. Or a task that has been frustrating for you. Take a piece of your life and give it to God. Tell God you are giving it to Him, and in your heart, release it. Should the worry or thoughts of this area come back, say to yourself, "I give this to you, God." Then sit back, relax, and watch what happens. I tell you it is amazing what God will do for you when you release something entirely into His hands with trust and faith. God is faithful, and He desires for us to have faith and trust in Him. When God sees that you have put your trust in Him for this thing or circumstance, He will move on your behalf.

As you practice this principle over and over, your ability to surrender will grow and grow. As your ability to surrender develops, you will begin to see God move in your life in more and more powerful ways. He will do things that you could not have imagined. He will give to you ideas and solutions you would have never imagined. It is more than worth it.

I love having everything figured out. I love it when a plan works according to my design. I love it when people respond to me the way I think they should. This is very good, but it also sets me up for constant disappointment. I should make plans. I should have reasonable expectations, knowing as I surrender my plans to God, do my best while allowing Him to do His part, the results are much better than anything I might have dreamed up. Don't you want the same thing?

Trust and surrender choices. It is not about what you feel; it is what you decide to do. It means having the courage to take a risk. I

> **Trust and surrender are choices**

have often said that the power of choice may be the most powerful thing God has ever given to humanity. Think about it; your decisions have gotten you where you are today. There have been bad choices and good choices, but our personal preferences have directed our paths through our life. We could discuss the power of choice at great lengths because of the many decisions we make every day. We can choose to live according to God's plan, and this choice has fantastic benefits with it. Again, God is not going to force us. He is not going to manipulate us. He allows the opportunity to surrender. The choice is yours. The only question is, what choice will you make?

CHAPTER 6, IMPARTATION

The Scriptures say it is better to give than receive. But the universal truth is that I cannot give unless I have received it. I cannot give what I do not have. So, therefore, I need to receive something to give it away.

God has asked us to be givers, but the cool part is that God also is a giver, and He wants to give us so much more than we could ever give away. I have always been a generous person. Sometimes, because of my compassion, people have tried to take advantage of that. I have had friends, family, church members, and missionaries ask for money. Some did not understand when I did not give it to them. I would say, "I cannot give you what I do not have. When I have enough to give, I will share it with you. I promise."

The gifts of God can be imparted and given away. It is terrific to receive a gift, but it is even better to give a gift. But the divine order is to receive, and then you may give.

When I speak about the gift of prophecy, I believe it is the ability to hear God and relay what He said. To prophesy a word heard from the Lord, we must first be able to listen to what He is saying. I have always connected the gift prophecy with the ability to hear God's voice, which is something all believers should do. I wrote earlier that to hear God's voice is a sign that one is a believer. In theory, if hearing our shepherds voice is an indicator that we are a Christian, then all Christians, in my humble opinion, should be able to prophesy.

I do not think this skill comes automatically the moment we are saved, but I do know it can be taught and learned. The first step is to receive the gift. Scripture tells us to pursue love and earnestly desire spiritual gifts (I Cor. 14:1). Again, I do not believe our heavenly Father would ever ask us to desire something that He would never give us. So obviously, the first step is to desire the gift.

Hearing God's voice will change your life. Hearing God's voice will lead you into paths of success. It will lead you to contentment. It will lead you to your purpose and can save your life by protecting you from all the various traps Satan has put out for you.

It boils down to two choices. We can take control and do whatever we think is best, or we can humbly realize that there is a God in heaven who knows more than we do, who is smarter than we are and can direct us into a life that is much more than we could ever imagine.

Now to Him who is able to do far more abundantly beyond all that we ask or think, according to the power that works within us,
(Eph 3:20).

It is against our nature to trust something we cannot see. Our human nature wants to be in charge and to feel safe and secure. But I promise you it is false security. How many times in our life did we made mistakes and wish we could have gone back and done things differently. I am writing to you now if you hear God's voice clearly and follow His instructions, you are not going to make a mistake.

> It is against our nature to trust something we cannot see.

King David was an incredible warrior. He united the kingdom of Israel and the kingdom of Judah. David had fantastic success on the battlefield. The key to his success was that he received instructions from God before he went to battle. He would ask God, "What do you want me to do in this fight? How do you want me to handle this?" God would give him specific instructions that would guarantee success.

1 Sam 23:2 - *So David inquired of the LORD, saying, "Shall I go and attack these Philistines?" And the LORD said to David, "Go and attack the Philistines and deliver Keilah."*
1 Sam 23:4 - *Then David inquired of the LORD once more. And the LORD answered him and said, "Arise, go down to Keilah, for I will give the Philistines into your hand."*

In the above Scriptures, David asked God if he should fight the battle. My mother used to tell me, "Son, always choose your battles." There is a time to fight. There is a time to wait. There is a time to go another direction. King David had success because he did not go to battle unless the Lord told him to, and when he followed God's plan, he was guaranteed victory. David would not only ask the Lord if he should fight, but he would ask specifically how and where?

I am not saying that we should hear God's voice for merely going to war. If God's voice can deliver the nation of Israel and bring them success and prosperity, will the voice of the Lord not do the same for an individual who God loves so much that He was willing to sacrifice His only Son to pay the price for their freedom?

Every day we are faced with decisions, some small and insignificant, and some very important. God is interested in every decision we make. We can ask God anything, and He loves us so much He is always willing to give us an answer. Sometimes the answer is not what we wanted to hear. Sometimes it seems like God is not saying anything, which means wait.

Worldly people will think you are foolish for believing you can hear God speak. But throughout the history of man, God has clearly spoken to us. It is very foolish not to think that God still speaks. There is a Scripture that prophetically warned us about this problem:

1 Cor 2:14 - *But a natural man does not accept the things of the Spirit of God, for they are foolishness to him; and he cannot understand them, because they are spiritually appraised.*

People who are not full of the Holy Spirit and do not have the mind of Christ cannot comprehend what you are saying concerning God. They will think you are foolish or crazy. The truth is, they are the foolish ones. I warn you of this because it is natural to want to be accepted. But when you start walking in this very close relationship with God, you may not be popular or accepted among your worldly friends, but if you are in a healthy spirit-filled church, you be accepted and even celebrated.

Let us take a look at scriptural commandments for impartation:

1 Peter 4:10 - *As each one has received a special gift, employ it in serving one another as good stewards of the manifold grace of God.*

In this beautiful Scripture, there are two clear parts. The first part speaks of receiving a gift. The second part speaks of using the gift for each other. You cannot give someone something you do not own. So, we must receive spiritual gifts so we can use them to help one another. The Lord wants us to receive unique gifts, especially the gift of prophecy so that we can use it for the good of other people.

This Scripture speaks clearly of the principle of serving other people with spiritual gifts. 1 Cor 12:7 - *But to each one is given the manifestation of the Spirit for the common good.* Gifts of the Spirit are for the good of others. It is very selfish not to desire these gifts. But again, remember very clearly that the number one gift the Lord wants us to desire is the gift of prophecy, which is all about hearing God's voice.

1 Cor 14:1 - *Pursue love, yet desire earnestly spiritual gifts, but especially that you may prophesy.*

The Lord tells us to especially desire to prophesy, and then a few verses later, a more definite statement is made concerning the prophetic gift. 1 Cor 14:39 - *Wherefore, brethren, covet to prophesy, (KJV)*

Commonly in the body of Christ, people want the gift of healing and the gift of faith, but the clear command of Scripture is to desire and covet to prophesy. When we prophesy, we hear our Father speak, and say what He tells us to say, and hopefully, obey His word.

We are called to hear His voice and speak what He tells us to speak, and do what He tells us to do. That is what I mean when I say hear His voice and be His voice. I do not want us ever to be arrogant and imply we are the sole mouthpiece of God. We should speak as humble ambassadors of Christ. We are to be His witnesses and follow His instructions.

> The clear command of Scripture is to covet to propehsey.

To be imparted means to receive something internally. The Scripture says repeatedly that the Spirit of God gives us gifts:

1 Cor 12:11 - *But one and the same Spirit works all these things, distributing to each one individually just as He wills.*

The word for receiving a spiritual gift from the Holy Spirit is "imparted." Impartation comes in several ways. You can pray in the name of Jesus Christ and ask the Holy Spirit to come upon you and give you the ability to hear God's voice, or a fellow believer who has a gift such as prophecy, can lay his hands on you and pray for you to be imparted with this wonderful gift.

1 Tim 4:14 - *Do not neglect the spiritual gift within you, which was bestowed on you through prophetic utterance with the laying on of hands by the presbytery.*

In Paul's letter to Timothy, it says these gifts are bestowed upon the believer by prophetic utterance with the laying on of hands. Then the reader is encouraged not to neglect the gift. Individual gifts can be received, but they also are to be used. Over the years, I have observed believers who have spiritual gifts but refuse for some reason or another to use them, and the gifts disappear. God wants us to use what He has given us because it is for the good of the body of Christ. Not to use what God has given us is an act of selfishness.

The Scripture commands us to be imparted to receive spiritual gifts and then use spiritual gifts. Impartation is not mystical; it is a beautiful gift from God that He will gladly give to any believer who is willing to ask.

Impartation happens in many ways. Through my years of ministry in many group settings where I taught this principle, at the end of class, I would pray for an impartation of the Holy Spirit to come upon the students. I would ask the students to be still and to have an attitude of receiving something from God. My prayer would go something like this –"Heavenly Father, we thank you for this day. We give you all praise. Father, in the name of Jesus Christ, I asked the Holy Spirit to come now and impart upon each student the gift of prophecy. Holy Spirit, we invite you to come. We ask for this gift, and we receive this gift now. Lord, I ask you to open up our ears to hear. Open up our hearts to receive everything the Holy Spirit has for us. Holy Spirit, in the name of Jesus, come and fall on each person now. Touch them, Lord. Touch them now. All praise to the name of Jesus. Amen." The result of this prayer is powerful. Countless times I have observed the Holy Spirit fall upon groups of people and impart to them supernatural spiritual gifts. If you have the faith that is willing, I encourage you to go ahead, say this prayer. This principle does not use a formula. Just pray from your heart and ask God for the ability to hear His voice, especially for the gift of prophecy as Scripture commands us to do. I promise you it will change your life.

You may ask, "how do I know if I have received a gift?" Some people incorrectly wait for a special magical feeling. Some people say they can feel the presence of God. You may have a warm feeling or tingling sensation, or you may feel absolutely nothing. When you received a gift, the important thing is to believe you have received it and act in faith regardless of your feelings. Scripture does not tell us to be led by our emotions; we are to be ruled by faith. So, if you said the prayer and you know it is God's will for you to receive it. According to Scripture, and if you are saved, you have the gift.

A fundamental principle of faith is the principle of thanksgiving. Since the Bible tells us, faith is the hope of things not seen. We can logically say that we should offer God thanksgiving even before we experience the answer to our prayers.

Heb 11:1 - Now *faith is the assurance of things hoped for, the conviction of things not seen.*

If you asked God to be able to hear His voice and have the gift of prophecy, the appropriate thing to do is to thank Him for answering your prayer. It does not seem logical to thank someone for giving you something you have not yet seen, but God requires faith and trust, and that is what you are doing when you thank Him before you see your answer.

I encourage you to practice. Yes, I said practice. Scripture refers to this as "stirring the gift that is within you" (2 Tim 1:6). For example, pray to God and ask questions, then get very still and pay attention to any voice or thoughts that pop into your mind out of nowhere.

So many times, His voice is simply an impression. Sometimes it is a picture. For me, usually, it is a thought that comes from nowhere. It is not something I would typically think.

I encourage my students to practice in small ways. Ask God a simple question. Perhaps something silly like, " Lord, where are my car keys?" Then practice listening. Yes, He cares about you enough that He will tell you where your car keys are. The point is to practice hearing His voice in small ways to help you learn how to recognize His voice and be able to listen to Him in critical matters later on.

Here is some practical advice on hearing God. Pay attention to your first impressions. Pay close attention to thoughts that are not normal for you. Pay close attention to creative ideas that are much more than you would

> I encourage my students to practice in small ways.

ever think. Also, pay close attention when a person or a face seems to pop into your mind and then thoughts and perhaps words concerning that person. I guarantee you it is time to pray for that person. There is a reason that a person came into your mind. Many times, the words that follow the picture of that person are a message from God that He wants you to deliver to them.

It is exciting when you have what you believe is a prophetic word for a person, and you give it to them, then they respond in a positive way asking, " how could you possibly know this?" It is time to give credit to God and use this moment as a faith builder for you and the person that received the word. It is incredibly encouraging. When a person knows that God is thinking about them and cares enough about them to speak to them through another person, it is truly a life-changing experience, and you can be a part of it.

The prophetic gift is enjoyable and extremely powerful when used correctly. And let me emphasize that nobody is perfect. We still have our normal tendencies and our imagination. Our analytics will get in the way, as well as our practical thoughts. But in the midst of it, God can still have His way and even speak and change your life and the lives of people around you,

In the coming chapters, I am going to talk more about how to recognize God's voice and get our natural tendencies out-of-the-way. My prayer is that you will be encouraged by this book, and have your desire increased for this gift. My hope is for you to be able to hear God's voice and perhaps change the lives of those around you. The impact first will be felt with you; then, it will affect your family and possibly your community, your church, and even our nation. That is how powerful this gift is!

CHAPTER 7, ACTIVATION

"Wherefore I put thee in remembrance that thou stir up the gift of God, which is in thee by the putting on of my hands." (2 Tim 1:6)

Apostle Paul reminded us to stir up the gifts given us, with an admonition to use it. The act of stirring is action. Action requires a choice on your part.

Here is a practical example of stirring. I am a tall man. I am 6 foot 4 inches in height. I have always been physically strong. One of my favorite hobbies is golf. I love to play for exercise and to clear my mind. I call it my mental break. I could always hit a golf ball far. There are periods when I do not get a chance to play. Returning to the game after taking a break, I find I do not hit the ball nearly as far nor as accurately. If I am playing with friends, they will ask me, "Hey, when is the last time you played?" They have noted my skills have diminished. I respond that I have not played golf for several weeks or months. Because I have not practiced my golf game, I do not play nearly as well. My fun-loving friends usually say something like "excuses, excuses." It is the same with spiritual gifts. If you do not exercise and stir up the gifts, the operation of the gifts will not be reliable or as strong.

God expects us to use what He has given us. He has imparted gifts to us for a reason. It concerns the benefit of those around us. Know that the gifts of God can be life or death for some people. The gifts of God contain blessings, warnings, healing, direction, confirmation, peace, and love.

> God expects us to use what He has given us

To stir up the gift means to use it. God has a purpose in everything that He does. The gifts have a divine purpose. God has given you a spiritual gift for a reason, and

He expects you to use it as much as possible. God desires for us to be faithful with everything He has given us. God is continually looking for committed Christians. I am not perfect at this, but I want to be known as a faithful Christian.

I heard a story recently about a young woman who dreamed of being an action movie star. The problem was she did not look like an action movie star. She was a little overweight and out of shape. When I go to the movies, action movie stars are usually physically fit. Yet this young woman was determined to be an action star. She believed this was her destiny. So, she went to the gym and began to work out. She did this every day for months until she finally transformed her appearance and felt prepared to be an action movie star. Soon after that, she landed the role of an action star in a major motion picture. If only Christians would work that hard to prepare themselves for their purpose. Countless times, I have heard Christians tell me they feel a call to be a pastor or an evangelist or missionary, yet they make no preparation. When God calls us to do something, He expects us to get ready. God has beautiful plans for us, but His plans always involve our participation. When we know what God has given us or what God wants us to do, we must pour ourselves into it and prepare ourselves in every possible way. I have witnessed several people who planted churches and began to pastor with no training. After a time, the church suffered because of poor Bible teaching, and members suffered from the pastor's limited ability to be a competent counselor. This is not intended to criticize churches or pastors. It is a principle of God that whatever He gives us to do, He expects us to train ourselves, get equipped, and be ready when ministry opportunities arise.

> God expects us to get ready for our call.

It is the same principle concerning spiritual gifts. When God imparts a gift to us, He expects us to use it. The best way to use it is to learn about it, get equipped, and trained. When I first started receiving spiritual gifts, I was advised by a mature Christian to go to a particular church where spiritual gifts were taught, and would I would be trained to grow in them. I went to that church as soon as I could. I thank God I was able to find a church moving in spiritual gifts. This enabled me to use the gifts God gave me. They taught me how to mature and grow in my gifting. Being in the right environment with the right leadership in the right church is critical.

A word about the naysayers - It is grievous how many well-meaning intelligent church leaders ridicule and deny anything supernatural. It seems anytime a believer claims to have experienced or moved in the supernatural, there will be a naysayer to tell them that cannot be from God. These people claim to be Bible supporters. They will take a scripture out of context to support their position. They need to read their Bible closer. The Bible is clear that signs and wonders will follow those that believe (Mark 16:17,18).

Jesus said those who believe in Him will do the same works that He did (John 14:12). Jesus said we shall receive power when the Holy Spirit comes upon us, and we will be His witnesses (Acts 1:8). Throughout the New Testament, there are stories of ordinary people performing supernatural signs in the name of Jesus. People like Philip, Peter, John, James, and Paul. Also, a group of believers who prayed for Paul when he was stoned and left for dead. The Scripture says Paul stood up, walked, and continued his ministry (Acts 14:19-20).

When a miracle occurs through a believer's action, it happens through the power of the Holy Spirit, who is glorifying Jesus Christ. It is the power of Jesus Christ residing by His Spirit in the temple of our body that allows us to do miracles. The credit does not go to the believer; the credit goes to Jesus Christ, our Savior. The Bible declares that our body is a temple of the Holy Ghost (1 Cor. 3:16). It is the Spirit of God who does the signs and wonders to bring glory to Christ. The Bible is clear on this. It is a shame that many people teach the Bible and ignore scriptures about the supernatural performed by ordinary believers. If a person claims to be a believer,

A believer must accept the whole New Covenant

they should accept the whole New Covenant, not just what their lack of experience teaches them. It is incomplete theology when a person does not understand Scripture because they have not experienced it.

CHAPTER 8, THE RIGHT SIDE OF THE CROSS

Through the years working in prophetic ministry, I noticed several classifications of prophetic people. The classification I prefer is what I call "New Covenant Prophets." These ministers clearly understand the finished work of Jesus Christ. Their prophetic words are in alignment and agreement with Jesus Christ and what He accomplished for us in His ministry, His death, and His resurrection. It is critical to understand God sees His people through the finished work of His beloved Son, Jesus. Our ministry must reflect this perspective and viewpoint. Jesus changed the world through His completed work on the cross and subsequent resurrection. All ministry must be in agreement with what Christ has done.

Unfortunately, I have run across many immature people who have a gift but have perverted it. I refer to those prophetic people as ones who prophesy on the wrong side of the cross. Their prophecies contain judgment, legalism, condemnation, and shame. It is an immature and damaging use of the gift. It is sad to see the gifts of God counterfeited by naive people. Some ministers may use the gift for personal gain. Many ministers prophesy on the wrong side of the cross out of ignorance. The wrong side of the cross refers to our status before Christ took our sins, shame, and condemnation upon His own body.

Unfortunately, the gifts of God can be perverted.

Having a clear understanding of the finished work of Jesus Christ is critical. It is the rule and the standard we used to respond to God's voice. It is difficult to have a standard if you do not know the standard. A minister does not have to be an expert in theology and have countless scriptures memorized. A minister who claims to be speaking, God's message must clearly understand the overall intent of Scripture. We must know the author of the Bible and understand His complete message. Violations of the message in Scripture will never be God's voice. God will never contradict what His Son accomplished. Jesus was part of a divine plan. The plan was perfect and complete. When we minister the word of God, we must agree with God's plan, as presented in the Bible. Let me give you an example. Consider this very famous passage:

> *"He is despised and rejected of men; a man of sorrows, and acquainted with grief: and we hid as it were our faces from him; he was despised, and we esteemed him not. Surely he hath borne our griefs, and carried our sorrows: yet we did esteem him stricken, smitten of God, and afflicted. But he was wounded for our transgressions, he was bruised for our iniquities: the chastisement of our peace was upon him; and with his stripes we are healed."* (Isaiah 53:3-5).

Jesus was punished, so we are forgiven. He was chastised for peace. Peace refers to us having peace with God. Jesus was wounded so we are healed. *"he hath borne our griefs, and carried our sorrows."* (Isaiah 53:4). This section translated in Hebrew - "carried sickness and endured our pain." Jesus, therefore, has taken our sickness away and endured our suffering and pain. *"and with his stripes we are healed."* (Isaiah 53:4). Jesus was wounded for our healing. This passage confirms Isaiah was speaking clearly about physical healing:

Jesus was wounded for our healing.

"When evening came, they brought to Him many who were demon-possessed; and He cast out the spirits with a word, and healed all who were ill. This was to fulfill what was spoken through Isaiah the prophet: "HE HIMSELF TOOK OUR INFIRMITIES AND CARRIED AWAY OUR DISEASES." (Matthew 8:16-17).

A prophetic word that speaks of God punishing you or God causing sickness to come on you is a clear violation of what Jesus accomplished. God will never undo what Jesus did. As believers in Jesus Christ, His finished work belongs to us. It is our legal inheritance. A prophetic word contradicting our inheritance as a believer is not coming from God. The only other two sources of that word is a person's imagination, or it is demonic.

This is not to suggest you have to be an expert theologian to determine if God is speaking to you or not. It is the knowledge of Jesus Christ and what He accomplished for you that assists you in deciding what God is saying to you. If someone speaks a word that has shame or condemnation in it, it is not coming from God. Jesus took our shame and received our condemnation. If someone speaks a prophetic word to you condemning you for a sin that was forgiven, it is not from God.

> **God will never undo what Jesus did.**

"If we confess our sins, He is faithful and righteous to forgive us our sins and to cleanse us from all unrighteousness." (1 John 1:9).

You should never accept as a prophetic word anything that brings up the guilt and shame of a past sin you have already confessed and ask forgiveness. A message of this sort is not the Lord speaking to you.

Sometimes well-meaning ministers inadvertently place condemnation on someone. Pointing out a fault must only have love as a motivation. Some people want to prove they are aware of your "fault." The purpose is not love but antagonism. Jesus took our condemnation to the cross. He was condemned as a criminal even though He was completely innocent. This condemnation was not His own; it was the condemnation that is due all of us because all have sinned against God (Rom 3:23). Because Jesus took condemnation upon Himself, if you are still feeling condemnation, it is not coming from God. This Scripture speaks of the finished work of Christ:

"Therefore, there is now no condemnation for those who are in Christ Jesus." (Rom 8:1).

The Apostle Paul, when he wrote his letters, understood what Christ had done. There is no condemnation upon a believer. To be perfectly clear, I may not feel condemnation; however, I can feel very convicted. The Holy Spirit has a powerful way of convicting us of sin. Being convicted when we have done something wrong and needing to repent and ask forgiveness is entirely different than carrying condemnation. *"And He, when He comes, will convict the world concerning sin and righteousness and judgment;"* (John 16:8). The Holy Spirit nudges us or gives us a little prick in our spirit when we need to make a change.

Remember, if Jesus died for it and you are a believer, it does not belong to you. This principle will always help you discern if God is speaking to you. God will not talk to you about - shame, condemnation, guilt, judgment, disease, unworthiness, curses, rejection, or anything concerning your old way of life before you were saved. All of those things were taken away by Jesus when He was on the cross.

In conclusion, prophecy needs to come from the right side of the cross. Everything changed when Jesus went to the cross and rose from the dead. God speaks to us from this perspective. God sees us through the accomplished work of Christ. He does not see us as unequal or unqualified. God sees us as joint-heirs with His Son. He does not see us as weak and pitiful, full of shame, guilt, and condemnation. The Lord sees us as forgiven and righteous now. We are His beloved children in right standing with Him. When He speaks to us, He speaks to us as a son or daughter in good standing. He speaks to us as a loving Father who loves us unconditionally and always has our best interest in mind. This is how our Heavenly Father speaks to us. When you understand this, it will help you know when God is talking to you.

> **Prophecy must come from the right side of the cross.**

CHAPTER 9, RESPONDING TO GOD'S VOICE

"Then in the midst of the assembly the Spirit of the LORD came upon Jahaziel the son of Zechariah, the son of Benaiah, the son of Jeiel, the son of Mattaniah, the Levite of the sons of Asaph; and he said, "Listen, all Judah and the inhabitants of Jerusalem and King Jehoshaphat: thus says the LORD to you, 'Do not fear or be dismayed because of this great multitude, for the battle is not yours but God's." (2 Chron 20:14 -15).

When God speaks, your response is essential. It can determine the outcome of a prophecy. I love the story in 2nd Chronicles beginning at the verse above. An utterly unknown person stands up in the crowd, hears the voice of God, and speaks a proclamation, saving a nation. When he spoke the declaration, it was important for King Jehoshaphat and his people to respond. God's word from this unknown person carried specific instructions that guarantee their success if they followed them. Notice I say if they followed directions, they would have victory.

Your response is essential.

Several nations had become allies to destroy Israel. The army facing them was fearsome. The King called for his people to pray. They were very distressed, but God spoke from an unlikely source, giving them encouragement and instructions.

The first instruction was: do not be afraid because this battle belongs to the Lord. The second instruction: what to expect and what they were to do. *"Tomorrow go down against them. Behold, they will come up by the ascent of Ziz, and you will find them at the end of the valley in front of the wilderness of Jeruel."* (2 Chron 20:16). The nation of Judah was instructed to go against them tomorrow - not today or next week - but tomorrow. God told them where the enemy would be and gave them more instructions. *"You need not fight in this battle; station yourselves, stand and see the salvation of the LORD on your behalf, O Judah and Jerusalem.' Do not fear or be dismayed; tomorrow go out to face them, for the LORD is with you."* (2 Chron 20:17).

They were not to fight, but station themselves in a specific place on this particular day. The Lord told them to position themselves at the end of a particular valley. This location was in front of the Wilderness of Jeruel. This is where they were to stand the next day. The instructions were precise. God had a plan and had given a prophetic word, but Israel needed to obey what God said.

It would have been easy for them to run and hide or to try to attack the enemy with a surprise move. Fortunately for them, they did what God asked them to do. The only thing they added was praise and worship. We know the rest of the story. God defeated all of the enemies in front of them.

It is clear when God speaks, our response is crucial. Years ago, before I was in ministry, I attended an early morning prayer meeting. There was a young lady there who had a powerful prophetic gift. At that time, I did not fully understand prophetic gifting, but her gift was very evident. One morning I entered a home for a prayer meeting. She looked at me and said I see the word "Pastor" written across your forehead. I thought it a bizarre thing to say. Should I have looked in the mirror to see if I had something smudged on my head that resembled the word "Pastor?" She was speaking what she heard the Lord say to her. Over the next few years through a series of events, I attended Bible College and was able to work to the doctorate level and eventually was sent out to Pastor a church in

West Tennessee. I always remembered the prophetic word that was given to me several years earlier in that prayer meeting. Fortunately, when the door opened, I was able to walk through it. I knew I had instructions from God, and this is what I was supposed to do.

Jesus told His disciples. *"I will tell you what is to come to pass, so it comes to pass you may believe."* (John 13:19). Often when God speaks, it is a foretelling of the future to prepare us for something He has in store for us. But even so, we still must respond. We have free will, and we can choose not to follow His instructions. I could have turned down the opportunity to pastor the little country church. I could have decided never to go to Bible College. I could have chosen to stay in the business world. Fortunately, I made choices in alignment with what God had given me through His word.

We should respond to prophecy. Our response can be simply one of gratitude and praise. Our response may be doing something specific God has asked us to do. Some prophecies are unconditional. These prophecies contain things God has promised that are going to happen. Many times, when God speaks, obedience is the only response. I have heard people say in the past the prophecy they received never came to fruition. I usually wonder if they obeyed what God asked them to do. Or was there another unmet condition? God can call you to something definite and tell you what it is, but if you do not respond, follow His instructions and obey Him, it does not mean the prophecy was not right. It means you disobeyed His will.

> I could have chosen to continue my career in business.

Many years ago, while I was in college, I was in what religious people call a "backslidden" state. I was a Christian, but I was not living a Christian lifestyle. I was living a party life. My primary purpose was having fun. It was a time in my past I have lived to regret. Amazingly, the Lord never took His hand off me even though I was living a sinful life at that point. While attending a party at an upstairs apartment, I was sitting with some friends listening to music and smoking marijuana. I do not remember everything thoroughly, but while I was sitting there, I had a powerful impression come over me that I needed to run away from there. The feeling was a strong sense of fear that seemed to overshadow me. In my heart, I knew I needed to get out of that place quickly. At the time, I did not know where the overwhelming sensation originated, but I could not deny it. I told my friends, "I've got to get out of here you, should get out of here too." They looked at me like I was crazy. Why would you want to leave? We are having a good time. I said again, "I just need to leave, and you should leave too." I got up to walk out of the apartment. As I was leaving, a group of men walked into the apartment. I remember feeling that something was wrong with these guys. There was a sense of evil about them. I continued walking out and went home.

I found out the next morning those men who entered the apartment as I was leaving, started violently beating people, and threw several people off the balcony. Later, people said the apartment looked like a war zone. The furniture was in pieces, and there was blood all over the walls. I had escaped, but now I know it was God protecting me, telling me to leave. When God speaks, it can be vital to respond.

> I know it was God protecting me.

God loves us very much. We are His children. Sometimes He speaks to us to fellowship and to express His love for us. Sometimes He speaks to us to direct us. Sometimes He speaks to encourage us. Sometimes He tells us things that are life-changing and critical for our future, and sometimes He tells us things that are about everyday life. What God wants from us is to be able to recognize His voice and to respond to Him. This is what a loving relationship is all about. I believe this is a learned behavior and that we can all discern His beautiful voice even better.

I have never met a mother who could not recognize the voice of her child calling out even in a crowded playground. The mother has trained her ear to know her child's voice. We, too, can train our ears to recognize the beautiful, incredible sound of our loving Father. The benefits of doing this are huge. It can mean the difference between success and failure and even life or death. God is as interested in small things in our life as He is in big situations.

Jesus paved the way for us to have a relationship with God. It is a Father-son relationship. To read about God, our Father is great, but being able to hear Him is even better. God wants to have a relationship with us. Every relationship requires communication. It is not just one person doing all of the talking, which is what so many of us do. We pray and petition God, but we do not always listen to His response. Prayer should be a two-way conversation, not a one-way requisition.

I believe we make hearing God's voice too complicated. Scripture is explicit, God is our loving Father. Every loving Father wants to speak to his children. God loves us more than we could ever imagine. He wants to be involved in our life. He wants to help us, assist us, teach us, and care for us. I have two natural-born children and two children by marriage and three grandchildren. I love to talk to my children and grandchildren. My children are older; they are adults living their own life, but I still want to talk to them and offer them any help I can. Like many parents, it can be frustrating because I know if they would carefully listen to me, I could save them a lot of pain and frustration. Often, I have to be still and let my children learn the hard way. I know if they had listened to me and had humbled themselves, it would have been much easier for them. Everyone seems to want to have their way.

The first thing we must do is have a solid belief our all-powerful, loving heavenly Father knows what is best for us. He has an answer for every problem. He will direct us in a path leading to our benefit. Living without His instruction sets us up for self-made difficulty.

Some will tell you that God only speaks through the written word of the Bible. I agree God speaks to us clearly through the Bible, and the Bible carries instructions for life. The concept of limiting God to only the Bible is illogical. I have four children, whom I have written texts and emails, and in the past old-fashioned letters. I hope my writings were beneficial to them. What would my relationship be with my children if I was not able to speak to them audibly? I love to write to my children and I think it is terrific when they read my words. I authored the book "Redeeming Your Past and Finding your Promised Land." I have written over four hundred Bible College courses, along with blogs, and various posts. I think it is great when my children choose to read my writing. But how would they know me if they did not spend time and have quality conversations with me? It is the same with God. God wants us to read His Word, but He also wants to speak to us and engage in a one-on-one personal relationship requiring conversation.

> Some say God only speaks through the Bible.

A thought about conversation, some people have the habit of not listening to what you say. They look at you as you speak, but what they are doing is formulating their response instead of considering what you are telling them. That is not a healthy conversation. In a healthy discussion, one person speaks, and the other person listens. The other person may ask a clarifying question and then formulate their response. I have noticed in some conversations, people want to speak, yet do not want to listen. I have several friends and one family member like that, and honestly, sometimes I dread talking to them. A healthy conversation requires give-and-take. A good discussion involves speaking clearly and listening carefully. In a healthy discussion, we value the other person's words and hope that they will also appreciate ours. So many times with God, we pray, say "Amen," and go about our business. Healthy communication involves speaking and listening. When you pray, if you will take time after you have talked to God to be still and listen, you will be surprised how many times He will speak to you. Instead of quickly ending your prayer with an amen, end your prayer with silence and a listening ear. I think you will much enjoy the benefits.

CHAPTER 10, HOW TO KNOW IF IT IS GOD SPEAKING

The million-dollar question is: "how can I be sure that it is God speaking to me"? I believe God has spoken to me many times, and I have not heard him. It is funny, my wife accuses me of the same thing. She says she has asked me to do something and I did not do it. In other words, I didn't hear my "honey-do." I was probably watching a football game and not paying attention. It is the same principle with us hearing God. Sometimes when God speaks to us, we are distracted and not listening. It must be very frustrating to God. It is amazing how much patience He has with us. He is patient because He loves us very much. It is just like my children, who can frustrate me and test my patience, yet, I continually have patience because I never stop loving them.

How can we be sure that it is God speaking to us? I believe, like so many things in life, it is trial and error. There were times when I honestly thought God was speaking to me, but He was not. I know there were times He talked to me, and it just went right over my head. Looking back over my life, when I made mistakes, I remember an inner voice trying to warn me, but I did not heed it. I know now if I had listened and obeyed, it would have saved me from the mistake.

> There was an inner voice trying to warn me.

Twenty Keys and Principles about God's Voice -
1. God's voice will never violate scriptural principles.
2. God's voice is usually something you would never think of yourself.

3. God's voice is loving.

4. God's voice does not contain condemnation or shame.

5. God's voice causes conviction.

6. God's voice can come in the form of a vision or mental picture.

7. God's voice can be words or impressions entering your mind out of nowhere.

8. God's voice will be a confirmation of something He has been trying to tell you all along.

9. God's voice can be an overwhelming feeling.

10. God's voice can be a gentle nudge.

11. God's voice can be an answer to a direct question.

12. God's voice can come through an unexpected divine appointment.

13. God will speak through a series of circumstances.

14. God will speak through a song.

15. God's voice can be heard through a sermon.

16. God speaks through dreams.

17. God's voice can be heard through an outward sign.

18. God's voice can be a sudden thought.

19. God speaks audibly.

20. God's voice can pop out of Scripture directly to you.

It is safe to say that God wants us to listen to Him.

God will speak some very unusual or seemingly illogical things. Years ago, I was young in the ministry and trying to get my school started. I had decided to name the school "The School of the Prophets" because that was the only school I found mentioned in the Bible. Samuel had a school of the

> God will speak some unusual things.

prophets in Scripture (1 Sam. 19:20). I was leasing space in an office building. This building contained a large conference room that I planned to convert into a classroom. I was very excited about starting a school. As I was praying about it, I felt or heard God say to begin the class on a particular day, but I was not to advertise it or promote it. I thought to myself that is strange, but fortunately, I was able to believe that God was speaking to me.

The night of the class came, and I faithfully set up my chairs and my podium and my sound system. I had a printed handout for each student. I had a registration table with literature all set up. The class was to begin at 7 p.m. I was nervous because I had not promoted this class. As the time approached, I was a little uneasy, but I had a peace within my heart about this class. I was not sure why I felt so peaceful. It was not logical to host an event and not tell people about it. At 7 p.m. as class was beginning, there were thirty people in the room. More showed up late. I was beside myself with excitement. I was able to ask a few of the students how they knew about this class, and everyone told me that the Lord had told them to come. This beginning class was a supernatural event.

It became apparent to me why God did this. It did not make logical sense, but it made Godly sense. Had I advertised and promoted this class and the people came; it would have been an accomplishment by Ray Self. I did not push this class, and people came anyway. This showed me this was God's class; He gets the credit and the glory. This is the way it should be in our life.

It made Godly sense.

If we let God have His way and listen to His voice, He will always do more than we expect. I was only expecting a handful of people, but forty people showed up, and they continued to show up every Monday night for over seven years. Only God could orchestrate something like this. It began by merely hearing God's voice.

What is the sound of His voice? As best I remember, when I prayed, I had this thought pop into my mind, "Do not advertise this class. Just wait." That thought was God's voice speaking to me, and it taught me a lesson that I never forgot.

Even with our best intentions, no one ever perfectly hears God. However, we can train ourselves to listen to Him better and better. It takes practice and a willingness to make mistakes. The only people who never fail are people who never try to do anything. The same principle goes with hearing God's voice. There will be failures. There will be times when you will completely miss it; those times can be our best teacher. I have probably learned more from my failures than I have through successes. When we miss God's voice, we may look foolish for a short time, or it may cause us to doubt, but it is worth the risk. The reward of being able to hear God is so great, it is worth everything we can do to acquire and cultivate our "God ear."

CHAPTER 11, BE HIS VOICE

"You will also decree a thing, and it will be established for you; And light will shine on your ways." (Job 22:28).

Please heed this word of warning. When I say to be His voice, I am not talking about a person who arrogantly claims to be "the" voice of God. This prideful and deceitful statement is not from God. There are many ways we can be His voice. One obvious way is by following His instructions and obeying what He is telling you to do. In this way, we become the manifestation of His voice. We can become His voice by living a Christian lifestyle and being a Godly example. We become His voice when we preach a sermon that touches the hearts of people. We become His voice when we love unconditionally, the way the Bible tells us to love. We become His voice by visiting the sick. We become His voice when we go on mission trips and spread the news of the Gospel to those who have not heard it. We become His voice when we do acts of kindness and spread His unconditional love. We become His voice when we share our testimony and allow people to choose salvation. There are many ways to be His voice.

> We become His voice when we do acts of kindness and love.

There are compelling scriptural principles to teach us about the power of proclaiming God's words. When we speak or do what God has asked us, we should expect powerful results. Speaking into the atmosphere anything we want does not necessarily produce anything. When you speak into the atmosphere what God tells you, you can expect something powerful to happen. The key is listening to God and following His instructions exactly.

'And Jesus answered saying to them, "Have faith in God. Truly I say to you, whoever says to this mountain, 'Be taken up and cast into the sea,' and does not doubt in his heart, but believes that what he says is going to happen, it will be granted him. Therefore I say to you, all things for which you pray and ask, believe that you have received them, and they will be granted you," (Mark 11:22 -24).

Jesus said to have faith in God and speak to the mountain and do not doubt, and it will move. He explains when we pray; we should believe. The obvious question is to believe what? The answer is: when we pray, we hear God speak because prayer is a conversation. We can believe our prayer will be answered. When we speak what we heard with faith, we will see the mountain move.

A mountain can be multiple problems. A mountain can be something that has been blocking your path for a long time. A mountain can be overwhelming circumstances or a problem with no answer. Jesus said we should pray and ask God about that situation, listen to what He says, believe what He says, and then speak. When we follow those principles, we can expect positive results.

I believe our words are powerful. When we speak in agreement with God, good things happen. When we speak in agreement with the devil and proclaim his lies, we can allow his demons to act. Our speech can be in covenant with God or agreement with the devil. Words come from our beliefs. Words impact our lives. Out of our mouth we can proclaim curses or blessings. *"from the same mouth come both blessing and cursing. My brethren, these things ought not to be this way."* (James 3:10). We can speak the truth, or we can speak lies. Our words can be in agreement with God, or we can speak in disobedience.

Our words are powerful.

We can speak positively or negatively. Speaking negative words attract negative things into our life. People who continually speak positive words tend to attract positive things to their lives. This is not to make a theological argument here; I am acknowledging what I have observed. When you read the Bible carefully, it all makes sense.

To be God's voice is about following Christ. Jesus made it clear that His sheep know His voice. In the Old Testament times, shepherds went to the sheep pens and called out to the sheep. The sheep belonging to the shepherd would follow him. The village typically would have a sheep pen with sheep belonging to many different shepherds. The sheep knew, by the sound of the voice, which shepherd they should follow. Jesus uses that principle to teach us to follow Him; we must know His voice. If we do not recognize His voice, we might follow the wrong shepherd. So how can I follow Jesus, be obedient to Him and live for Him, if I do not know His voice? Yes, again, His voice is the word of God, but my savior is still alive, and He still speaks to each one of us personally. Yes, He can talk personally through the Bible, but He also speaks to our hearts and our mind. Unfortunately, so many in our society think people who say they hear God are crazy. These people choose to ignore the Bible. It clearly teaches us God spoke to His people for thousands of years, and the sign of being a Christian is one that knows the voice of God. To be His voice is to hear His voice and obey Him, whatever instructions He gives you. It is to live for Him, to work for Him, and be an example of Him.

CHAPTER 12, THE PROPHETIC GIFT GIVES GLORY TO GOD

I recently ministered in the Pittsburgh area. I was blessed to be able to participate in multiple ministry events. One such event touched my heart. It was an area pastors' luncheon. My traveling companion and I were asked to speak and minister to the pastors who had gathered. We had lunch, and then the Pastor I was with spoke a short, encouraging word. We asked different pastors to come forward, so we could pray for them. One particular Pastor, known as Pastor Dan, came up front and sat in a chair next to me. I put my hand on his shoulder and began to pray for him. As I was praying for him, I saw a clear picture in my mind. It was like a short video clip. I saw a man walking down a very long rocky pathway. I could tell that he had been walking that path of a very long time. I sensed that his feet were exhausted. I saw in my mind a picture of a soft green pasture. Then I saw him walking across soft green grass. I knew from this vision this man had endured a long and challenging walk, but the Lord wanted to give him a time of healing for his feet. I shared this with him. Then he said something surprising. He told me, "you have no idea, but your vision is very accurate. My feet are exhausted. I am scheduled for a doctor's appointment for my feet this very afternoon."

I saw a picture in my mind.

The only way to explain this is the Lord had spoken and wanted to encourage this tired Pastor. Prophecy should always be to encourage and edify the individual (1 Cor. 14:3). This particular Pastor was edified and encouraged as well as everyone else in the room. Prophecy is a tremendous faith builder. Prophetic words give us comfort and let us know that God truly cares for us.

Events like this still completely amaze me and increase my faith. When I am ministering prophetically, there is always this little voice that says, "are you sure this is God speaking? Maybe it is just your imagination." Time and time again, I am utterly amazed that it truly is the Lord speaking by the responses I hear.

On the same trip, I received another testimony that profoundly touched my heart. A woman came up to me and said, you might not remember this, but you and your friend prayed over me six years ago and told me I was going to have a baby. It was hard for me to believe because I was not supposed to be able to have children. You said I was going to have a baby, and then my friend Joe Warner said, "yes, you're going to have two girls and a boy." I want you to meet my children, and she introduced me to her two beautiful little girls and her little boy. Things like this cannot be explained naturally. Something like this gives glory to our supernatural, wonderful, loving God. I did not feel a sense of pride when she told me this. I felt incredibly humbled and amazed at the goodness of God. I truly felt like I was going to start to cry right in front of her. Our God is incredible. The amount of love He has for us is almost incomprehensible. Prophetic ministry is just another way that God shows His great love and care for His children.

During another church service, I was asked to take the microphone and call people out from the audience who wish to receive prayer and if the Lord wills, a prophetic word. This can be very intimidating. It truly is a test of faith. It requires trust God is not going to let me down or the people in attendance. An older lady came up to me and asked me to pray for her. As I began to pray for her, I felt directed to pray about her blood sugar. I prayed that the Lord would return her blood sugar to normal levels, and I prayed that her pancreas would be healed in the name of Jesus. I was listening to the Lord as I was praying for His direction on how to pray. The lady began to cry. She cried so hard she could not stand up straight. She looked at me, and she took the microphone from my hand and told the church that just that afternoon, her doctor had diagnosed her with diabetes. She began to praise God with tears of joy. Despite her diagnosis, the Lord cared enough about her to direct me to pray for healing over her prophetically. The message was clear. God cared about her and knew what she is going through.

I believe the Lord wanted to heal her. I do not know the end of the story as I left town the next day. I am not even sure of her name. I do know this; her faith was increased tremendously. She received comfort, encouragement, and received hope. This is what the gift of prophecy is meant to do. It is designed by God to increase our faith in Him and to let us know how much He truly loves us. I know this event raised that woman's faith, gave her great comfort and encouragement. It also increased my faith and the faith of those in attendance that night.

I love real-life events because they destroy arguments. There is much disagreement over theology. Who is a correct teacher? Who is a false teacher? Which Church is the best? Why my belief is correct in yours is wrong. This sometimes makes an interesting discussion. What I love about stories is they relay an experience. There is no theological argument. I am not saying I am correct and you are wrong, or my way is better than your way. I am relaying what happened. I could be a person who makes up stories, but that would not be me. It is up to you to believe what I am saying or choose not to accept it. My part is to tell you what happened.

> Real-life events destroy arguments.

I was in a small church in South Mississippi very recently. I was blessed to be the main speaker. For the Sunday morning service, I love to get up and preach the word of God. I especially love it when I can sense His presence in the room. I love taking Scripture, making it real and applicable to my audience. God's word is so healing, so comforting, and so powerful. It is a privilege to be able to preach it. Whenever I get a chance to preach, I always feel incredibly blessed.

During my ministry time that weekend, I was asked to do a class on prophecy and divine order for the evening. My job was to teach on the prophetic gift. I spoke about how to use the gift in an orderly way under the authority of the church. If I talk about the prophetic gift, I always feel compelled to demonstrate the prophetic gift. God put it on my heart that I should never teach something I am not willing to do. As I was teaching about the prophetic gift, I felt drawn toward a lady sitting on the second row. Sometimes when ministering, I get a little silly, or as my wife says, I try to be funny. I have found over the years of ministry, using a little humor helps people to relax and makes whatever I am saying more interesting. Humor keeps people's attention. I said to the group, " who here would like to receive a prophetic word?"

Before allowing anyone to answer, I pointed my finger at the lady in the second row, and I said, "Oh, okay, you." She looked stunned. The expression on her face was like a deer in headlights. Her eyes opened very wide, and she seemed somewhat frozen. I said to her, "I promise it will not hurt you. It's okay," and I had a big smile on my face. I got very still for a moment, and I prayed in my heart, "Lord, please speak to me and give me a word for this young lady."

As I looked at her, I began to speak about things from her past, including her prophetic gifting. I do not remember everything I said to her. This is common in prophetic ministry. When a minister gives a prophetic word, it is not a message from him or for him, it is for another person. I cannot tell you how many times ministers have said to me after they give a prophetic word, they do not remember it much later. Well, the young lady just sat there very quiet. I went on teaching. At the end of the class, she came up to me, and she said, "You have no idea what just happened. Before I came to church tonight, I was praying to God and asking Him about the prophetic gift. I asked Him for a sign if I had this gift, He would single me out in class tonight. This is exactly what just happened to me through you." She had tears in her eyes. She asked me about a hundred questions. I still receive messages from her.

The prophetic gift does what the word of God says. It edifies, encourages, and gives comfort. I have found many times the prophetic word is simply a confirmation of what God's been trying to tell you all along. So many times, people receive a prophetic word, and it sounds very familiar to

> She asked God for a sign and the Lord used me to give it to her.

them. Usually, it is something that has been in their hearts for a long time, and they were struggling to understand if it was coming from God. Sometimes people dismiss a message and put it in the back recesses of their mind. At this point, the prophetic gift comes to remind and confirm to them what God has been trying to speak to them. It is compelling and an incredible blessing.

Prophetic ministry is encouraging and powerful. The body of Christ needs it. I think it has been made too bizarre and too weird when actually, it is something when appropriately handled should be normal for any Christian. Jesus made it clear His sheep know Him, and they hear His voice. If we are Christian, then we should have the ability to discern Jesus's voice. We should know God loves us, cares for us, and wants to encourage us and give us hope.

Prophetic words are not the only way He does this, obviously, but it is one of the most powerful ways the Lord encourages us.

I am a Christian counselor. I am very blessed to have a doctorate in Christian psychology. I can counsel and give the very best wisdom I can, but if I can give them one supernatural word straight from the heart of God, it will do more for them than years of natural counseling. Hearing God is a life-changing experience. God is speaking to all of us, but most of us are too busy to hear. Because God is merciful, He sends us another person to speak to us about what He has been trying to tell us all along.

"He will glorify Me, for He will take of Mine and will disclose it to you." (John 16:14). This verse is a key scripture to help us know if it is the Lord speaking. Jesus is telling us the Holy Spirit always gives glory to Him. This means if the Holy Spirit is doing something, he gives credit and acknowledgment to Jesus Christ, the Son of God. When I speak of prophetic testimonies, I intend to give glory to Jesus Christ. I always fear I may make a mistake and glorify myself. I know it is a dangerous and foolish thing to take credit away from God and accept it for yourself. Please understand that this is never my intent.

Sadly, many Christians have been traditionally taught to believe God does not use a believer to give a prophetic word. This is an insult to God and to His word, which says clearly through many scriptures God uses ordinary people to deliver prophetic words. Teaching God does not do this anymore does not change the truth. As I wrote earlier, the Bible tells us to desire the prophetic gift above all other gifts. *"Pursue love, yet desire earnestly spiritual gifts, but especially that you may prophesy."* (1 Cor 14:1). If a person will just read the word of God and let it speak for itself, he will see countless examples of God speaking to His children. The Bible tells us God is the same yesterday, today, and forever (Hebrews 13:8). It is illogical to believe that God quit speaking with the printing of the Bible. Please do not base your theology on your lack of experience.

I desire to take the gifting God gave me to encourage others with this gifting. Not only to assist others with my gifting but help them to operate in the Holy Spirit this way, also. God wants to speak to His children. He wants us to listen because He loves us. He wants us to obey Him because obedience to Him is what is best for us.

For so long, I felt obedience to God was going to be joyless, painful, and restricting. I did not realize obedience to God would do the opposite and bring me joy, abundance, and peace in my life. God wants us to hear and obey Him because He has amazing things in store for us. He does not want us to miss them. Just because you have not experienced this yet, it does not mean it is not real. You may not have experienced hearing God, and having your life changed as a result, but that does not change the reality God is speaking to you and has beautiful things waiting for you!

> Do not base your theology on your lack of experience.

CHAPTER 13, UNDER COVER - PROPHECY AND THE LOCAL CHURCH

Psalms 91:1 He *who dwells in the shelter of the Most High Will abide in the shadow of the Almighty.*

I have always loved scripture. I appreciate it when I learn precisely what it means culturally at a particular time in history. To correctly interpret the Bible, we should be aware of the audience and the timeline from when it was written. For example, Psalms 91, the first verse talks about abiding under the shadow of God. Culturally speaking, this refers figurately to being in God's home or tent. In Old Testament times, when a person was traveling with their family or friends, and they became tired, they would look for a home or tent to stay overnight. For instance, if they came upon a tent in the desert that looked like an excellent place to rest, they would come up to the shelter and grab hold of the tent cord. Traditionally the owner of the tent would invite them in as his guest. They would be abiding under his shadow. As long as the guest was in the home, the owner of the tent was responsible for their care. He will provide food a place to sleep and protection as long as they were abiding under his shadow. I love this principle. When we come to the Lord's House and come into His presence, we are abiding in His shadow, and He will provide for us and protect us. This is a beautiful picture of God's authority and provision.

Being under authority is a great place to be. Unfortunately, in the world's view to be under authority means to be controlled against your will. God's view of authority is an

> **Being under authority is a great place to be.**

excellent place for us to be because it gives us blessings, provision, and protection. Being under authority is for our benefit. It is not the wrong place to be. It is a great place to be. And what I love about being under authority is that the gifts of the Holy Spirit, when submitted to proper authority, tend to grow and expand beyond anything we could imagine. It takes humility and a willingness to lay down your agenda at times, but it is well worth that minor sacrifice. Look at the rest of the promises of this scripture -

> Psalms 91:2 - 6 I *will say to the LORD, "My refuge and my fortress, My God, in whom I trust!" For it is He who delivers you from the snare of the trapper and from the deadly pestilence. He will cover you with His pinions, And under His wings you may seek refuge; His faithfulnessis a shield and bulwark. You will not be afraid of the terror by night, or of the arrow that flies by day; Of the pestilence that stalks in darkness, Or of the destruction that lays waste at noon.*

I believe that the church is God's home. The church is the house of God. I think that respecting that institution and submitting myself to the church is hugely beneficial to us. I believe that God's authority on Earth is His church. I want to be a part of that church. Jesus said something exciting about the church. Truthfully, He told many exciting things. Jesus said that the gates of hell would not prevail against His church (Mat 16:18). Well, folks, I want to be in a place where the Gates of hell will not prevail. Don't you?

> I want to be where the gates of hell will not prevail.

The Bible has a lot to say about submission. Honestly, submission goes against our human nature. As I wrote in a previous chapter, we like to be in control. Submitting gives up a level of control. What I have learned, sometimes the hard way that submitting to authority opens up doors and opportunities that I could never imagine. My flesh or human nature tells me that submitting is going to cause me to be stifled and ignored. But actually, the opposite is true. Many times, I have to fight my tendency to want to be in charge and in control. I have always been a leader. There are instances that God tells me to lead, and I have to take that responsibility, but wherever I am, I submit myself to the local church. I am in submission to Freedom Fellowship Church of Orlando, Florida. It has not been hard at all. I cannot tell you that I always agree with everything the church does, but I can honestly tell you that since I submitted myself to this church, doors and opportunities have opened up for me that I could have never ever imagined.

As I mentioned earlier in this book, when I moved from Memphis, Tennessee to Orlando, Florida, I had a significant ministry. I could have taken the attitude that this little local church in Orlando should submit to my ministry. But I knew immediately that is not what God wanted me to do. I submitted myself and my ministry to this church, and I am happy that I did. I had to humble myself. I was accustomed to being a senior pastor and the one that made the major decisions about the church, but that was no more. However, by submitting to this church's authority, opportunities opened up for me to travel to cities all over the United States and minister. I have been part of mission teams to the Philippines, Indonesia, Guatemala, and Spain. The ministry the Lord gave me to manage for Him has indeed become international. While I was under the authority of the church, I was blessed to be the leader in building a genuinely International Bible College with a website that contains over 1,400 internet pages and a school that is accredited and full of the Holy Spirit. It is a dream come true that only God could orchestrate. And I know that part of it was because of the submission to the local church.

Sadly, many people with prophetic gifting have trouble with submission. I have known many people with this gift to have a great spirit of revelation. They genuinely hear from God and have a profound revelation of His word. But when the local church does not seem to appreciate their revelation, they get easily offended and do not hang around very long. These people tend to float from church to church, looking for the place where their gifting will be genuinely appreciated. It is actually a demonic trap. The people who float around not under authority have ministries that generally do not have much impact or success.

> **Many people with the prophetic gift have trouble with submission.**

God gave me a simple solution to this. The answer is for the revelation of the prophet to always submit to the wisdom of the pastor. God gives faithful pastors the knowledge to lead the church and determine its direction. It takes a tremendous amount of Godly wisdom to have an effective church service. Prophetic people do not always understand that. They just cannot seem to understand why the pastor will not stop the service and let them demonstrate their gift. What they do not realize is that God speaks to pastors differently than He talks to prophets. Throughout Biblical times God spoke to the leaders differently than He spoke to other people. I may not understand why a pastor is doing what he is doing, but I need to be able to trust that he has heard something from God that I know nothing about. Often it takes a lot of humility.

The bible is very clear on the subject of submission. Consider the following scriptures:

Romans 13:1 Every *person is to be in subjection to the governing authorities. For there is no authority except from God, and those which exist are established by God.*

Ephesians 5:21 *and be subject to one another in the fear of Christ.* Titus 3:1 *Remind them to be subject to rulers, to authorities, to be obedient, to be ready for every good deed,*

1 Peter 5:5 You *younger men, likewise, be subject to your elders; and all of you, clothe yourselves with humility toward one another, for GOD IS OPPOSED TO THE PROUD, BUT GIVES GRACE TO THE HUMBLE.*

Hebrews 13:17 Obey *your leaders and submit to them, for they keep watch over your souls as those who will give an account. Let them do this with joy and not with grief, for this would be unprofitable for you.*

When God repeats His commandments throughout scripture, they should be taken very seriously. Always remember that your Heavenly Father desires what is best for you. Submission to authority is not easy or natural, but it is for our good. When we willingly submit, we put ourselves in a position to be used by God in ways that we could never previously imagine.

CHAPTER 14, GOD SPEAKS DIRECTLY THROUGH SCRIPTURE

I have mentioned several times in this book that God speaks very clearly through His word. I want to give examples of how God speaks to us personally through the Bible. Now I realize there are always valuable life lessons to be learned from scripture, but that is not the same as a personal message. The Bible is no ordinary book. The Bible is God's word to man. It is powerful and life-changing. The Bible has proven itself for centuries to be accurate, infallible, and completely trustworthy.

This book, however, is a book about hearing God's voice and then becoming His voice as a witness of Christ to the world. One of the best ways to do this is to go to God's word and read it prayerfully. Before you read a particular chapter, pause and pray and ask the Lord to speak to you through His word. Sometimes if you will get still before you read the Bible, the Holy Spirit will direct you to what chapter or book he wants you to read. You may have an immediate impression that seems to come out of nowhere or a desire that radiates from your heart. Or it could be in your heart you hear God say, "turn to Isaiah chapter 40."

> Ask God to speak to you through His word (the bible).

The point is when you read the Bible, it is very common for God to speak to you personally. I frequently say that scriptures seem to jump off the page at me. I could read verse after verse and all of a sudden, I come to one particular verse and wham, it just gets to me, and I stop and reread it. I realize that it is God trying to tell me something.

Remember, God is always relaying His message to us through the Bible, but there are times when I need a personal message just for myself because I am looking for an answer, or I am not at peace in my heart, or I am struggling in a specific area.

Let me give you an example. As I am writing, I do not have a particular verse or chapter in mind. What I am going to do this moment is to get quiet and pray and ask God to guide me to what chapter or verse He wants me to write about. Okay, I prayed, and Matthew, chapter 18, seemed to pop into my head from out of nowhere. I have learned over the years to pay attention to those thoughts that seem to come out of nowhere. Remember, the Lord said, *"his thoughts are not our thoughts and his ways are not our ways"* (Isaiah 55:8). I turn to the chapter and read it very carefully. It starts off talking about becoming like a child and humbling ourselves to enter the kingdom of God, and then it moves on to how to handle a brother who is in sin. The chapter then speaks about forgiveness and also leaving 99 and going after the one. However, I felt drawn back to the first five or six verses about becoming like a child.

As I am writing this book, I have been going through some challenging struggles in my life. I have been praying and asking God for help like so many people do when they have troubles. I am not going to go into any detail right now about the specifics of those struggles. However, I feel the Lord is telling me something very directly. These verses seem to be to hold a personal message for me as I am writing –

Mat 18:1 - 4 *At that time the disciples came to Jesus and said, "Who then is greatest in the kingdom of heaven?" And He called a child to Himself and set him before them, and said, "Truly I say to you, unless you are converted and become like children, you will not enter the kingdom of heaven. "Whoever then humbles himself as this child, he is the greatest in the kingdom of heaven.*

I feel in my heart (which means this is not entirely logical) that God wants me to go a very deep level of trust. A young child trusts their parent completely. A young child may be upset or fearful, but they know Mama and Daddy are there, and they trust Mama and Daddy to take care of them. A child trusts his parents to give him what he needs. The child does not consciously think of these things. A child knows that he can trust his parents to take care of him. I believe God is trying to tell me I need to humble myself entirely and develop a childlike trust in Him during this difficult time.

As an adult, we generally think we have to take care of things. We need to fix it, handle it, solve it, repair it whatever it takes. God desires for me to completely let go and trust Him 100%. I know this sounds like a Sunday school lesson, but actually, it is challenging for an adult to completely let go I trust God. Most of us have too much natural pride and self-preservation to do that. But let go, and trust is exactly what God is asking me to do. I have learned this about our father in heaven, He will never ask you to do something that He will not empower you to do. So the first thing I must do is make a decision. Everything starts with the decision. Just a simple choice. I am deciding right now it is alright to humble myself, let go of my ways, and trust the Lord to handle what I am going through.

It is funny, but just writing this gives me peace. One of the beautiful things about our Lord is when He speaks to us, He gives us peace. This is something the devil cannot counterfeit. There is never any real peace when the devil speaks.

I am a teacher of the word of God. But I want to be more than a teacher I want to be a doer of the word. A doer is someone who says

I will not only teach the Bible, but I will do what it instructs and demonstrate biblical principles. The principle of doing is elementary but very powerful. God loves to speak to us through His previously written word. Through the Scriptures, God wants to tell us stories, teach us, and powerfully talk to us personally. I love to study the word and read the stories in the New and Old Testaments. I think that is important for all believers, but anytime I read, I am always paying attention to that tugging in my heart, where God wants to tell me something personally.

As a teacher and a preacher many times when reading the word, God gives me messages for a group or a church. That should be what any good preacher desires. There are thousands of life messages in Scripture. But what matters most is the message the group you are speaking to needs to hear.

As you read, learn to tune your spirit and your ear toward God. In a way, it is a form of multitasking. You are reading and listening at the same time. I love to do that. I actually do the same thing when I pray for people. I multitask when I am praying for another person. I am praying for them and listening at the same time for something God may want to say to them personally. You know we can teach and preach and write, but when God speaks personally to you, that changes your life like no other thing can possibly do.

> What matters is the message your audience needs to hear.

I encourage you to grab your Bible or your electronic device, pray, and ask the Lord to guide you through His word. You can ask God where He wants you to go in His word. Pay attention to those thoughts and impressions, and do not dismiss them. Go to the verses from your thoughts and feelings and read and listen. It will change your life. Amen

CHAPTER 15, MINISTERING PROPHETICALLY

John 14:10 *"Do you not believe that I am in the Father, and the Father is in Me? The words that I say to you I do not speak on My own initiative, but the Father abiding in Me does His works."*

When Jesus minister to people, He made it very clear that what He spoke was not coming from His own thoughts. In the above scripture, it is clear that Jesus was listening to His Father as He spoke. He was hearing God speak to Him and then relaying that message to the people He was ministering to.

He made it clear that His Father's Spirit lived in Him, and it was that spirit that was doing the works. This is a compelling principle. Jesus made it known that He was only following the instructions of His Heavenly Father. His words carry authority because they were not His words, but they were God's words. His actions or as He said His works were actually God's works. Jesus's ministry was full of the supernatural. He used the supernatural to build faith and established God's reality to His beloved children.

Jesus was in tune with His Father all the time. He knew His father's heart, and this intimacy empowered His ministry. This is what made Him the most influential person in the history of the world. Jesus spoke and acted according to what He heard His father tell Him to do.

Now here comes the part that trips most people up. As Christians, as followers of Christ, we are asked to do the same thing. This is beyond our capability. This is beyond our logic and reason. But this is precisely what we are asked to do. Jesus made it clear that the Father lived within Him. The Apostle Paul explained very clearly in his letter to the Corinthians that the Holy Spirit of God lives inside believers.

1 Cor 3:16 *Do you not know that you are a temple of God and that the Spirit of God dwells in you?*

This is the same spirit of God that lived inside of Jesus. It was the Holy Spirit that motivated Jesus. The Holy Spirit is God. The Holy Spirit lived inside of Jesus and was His initiator. The Holy Spirit also lives inside of Christians and should be our primary motivator.

The Holy Spirit is our motivator.

Scripture makes this perfectly clear when Jesus said something very astounding. John 14:12 *"Truly, truly, I say to you, he who believes in Me, the works that I do, he will do also; and greater works than these he will do; because I go to the Father."*

One of the works that Jesus is referring to is prophetic works. Prophetic Ministry involves listening to the Lord and ministering the way He wants us to minister. For ministry to be powerful, it has to be initiated by the Holy Spirit living within us. This is where the power of God will manifest itself. Prophetic ministry is incredibly powerful. Prophetic ministry brings the supernatural into the natural. Prophetic ministry brings glory to God and is an incredible faith builder.

I have said this before, and I will say it again. When I pray for a person, I try to always be in a listening mode. You may be praying for the person in front of you at the altar and listening to the Holy Spirit at the same time. Many times when I pray for another person, in the beginning, it is a very natural prayer. The prayer is just what I think should be said or petitioned. But as I pray, I have learned to pay attention to those thoughts and impressions that seemed to come out of nowhere. I have learned to open my mouth and begin to speak those impressions. Many times, the impressions do not become evident until the words are formed and expressed. I cannot tell you how many times amazing things have happened, and the person in front of me was incredibly blessed. When this happens, not only does my faith goes through the roof but the person receiving the prayer will believe like never before

Some people that received my prayer will ask me how I knew what I spoke. This is a common reaction to a person who has never receive prophetic ministry. I always give credit to God and no credit to myself or any unique ability that I may have. It is God who gets the glory because it is God doing the work. All He asked us to do is be His vessel and pay attention to what He is asking us to do and obey Him. This is demonstrated throughout scripture. The Bible is our instruction book. The author of the Bible lives inside us and is speaking to us almost continually. But I believe the author of the Bible, the Holy Spirit, especially loves to talk to us when we are trying to minister or bless another person. Many of us get so caught up in our own words that we blot out the impressions or words that God is trying to speak.

> The author of the Bible lives inside us.

Prophetic ministry is a skill that can be learned by practice. When I first make a new friend, their voice is new to me. When they call me on the phone, they need to identify themselves. However, after a few phone calls, they no longer need to identify themselves because I immediately recognize their voice. I have heard their voice before, and I know who it belongs to. It may sound like an oversimplification. The same principle works with God's voice. The more you practice hearing His voice, and the better you will become with voice recognition. Recognizing God's voice by distinguishing it from the other noises in your mind is a vital key for prophetic ministry.

CHAPTER 16, TEAM MINISTRY

1 Cor 14:29 *Let two or three prophets speak, and let the others pass judgment.*

1 Cor 14:31 *For you can all prophesy one by one, so that all may learn and all may be exhorted;*

Ministering as a team can be very powerful and extremely effective. Ministry with other people, however, can be challenging. This phrase "For you can all prophesy one by one. " is a crucial verse pointing to prophetic team ministry. In my church in Orlando, it is not unusual for the pastor to call the prophetic team to come forward to minister to various people. Our prophetic team is a group of men and women who have a proven track record with the prophetic gift. But ministering with a group of ministers can get out of order. Each member must be in sync with the other members of the group. When the group is ministering, and each one is tuned in to the Lord, there is a prophetic flow. It is like singing a song where everybody's in the same key singing with beautiful harmony. When a prophetic team is not in sync, it is like everyone is singing a song, but several people are off-key, and therefore, the song loses the appeal.

> It is like everyone singing the same song in the same key.

This is what I encourage concerning prophetic team ministry. First, do not overdo it. One thing that makes me somewhat nervous is when a crowd of people gathers around an individual, and everybody wants to pray over them. Now that is not necessarily a bad thing, but it can be a very confusing time. When ministers are in tune with the Holy Spirit, there is a beautiful flow. It is like the river of the anointing will flow from one person to the other. There is a definite theme and a particular message. It is not unusual for one minister to have part of the message then the second minister to pick up another piece and the third minister to pick up another part etc. There is a flow to the Holy Spirit, and there is harmony with the Holy Spirit that is critical. When ministering as a team, each member of the team should be aware of that flow.

One mistake I have witnessed is when several people are praying for an individual, and it is clear the third or fourth person who prays for that individual has not listened to anything that was said previously. It is like we are singing a song somebody walks up and starts singing something completely different. When that happens, it puts a cold blanket on what the Lord is trying to say.

In team ministry, each member of the team must be aware of what is being prayed by the other members. There should be an awareness of what the Holy Spirit is trying to do. The Holy Spirit is very orderly and is not going to cause confusion or keep changing the topic. The Holy Spirit wants to edify and encourage, and that cannot happen if there is disharmony among those performing the ministry.

Let me tell you a funny story (it is funny if you have my strange sense of humor). In my church, some years ago, all of the leaders would gather before each service, and we would stand in a circle, hold hands, and pray. It was always a significant time. We would pray for the upcoming service and for the members that would be attending. We would ask the Lord to have His way and other things such as that.

However, it seemed no matter what we are praying, one of my leaders, I will call him Mike, would start praying something entirely out of left field. It would go something like this. As a group, we would pray, "O Lord Jesus, we ask for your Holy Spirit to come and just bring healing to this congregation today. If there's anyone sick, we pray that you would touch them and heal their bodies. We ask you to bring comfort to the brokenhearted and encourage those in the church today who are suffering." Then Mike would say 'Lord, we pray for the refugees in Afghanistan that you would deliver them to Pakistan." There's nothing wrong with praying for the refugees in Afghanistan, but it really was not on topic. One day I pulled him aside and said, "Mike, when you pray, it is like we are all playing basketball, and you show up with a football. Or we are singing Amazing Grace and you start singing the National Anthem at the same time." What I was trying to tell him jokingly was, "Hey Mike, you got to get in sync with what the Holy Spirit is doing here.

In team ministry, it is imperative to listen to what the Holy Spirit is saying and try to stay in that vein. When that happens, it is absolutely amazing and beautiful. Every time I have been in a group that is in sync with the Holy Spirit, I would feel a unity and a flow that is in tune with what the Lord is trying to do. To be powerful, as I have written in previous chapters, we want to pray and say what the Lord wants us to pray and speak. Continually strive to listen to what has been said before it is your time to minister. That is going to give you a sense of what the Lord is doing and help you to hear God's voice even better.

Another tip I want to encourage you with is after a prophetic word is given by another person, and it is your turn to speak, do not be in too much of a hurry. Allow the recipient to digest what was just spoken to them before you give them something else to

Do not move too fast after a word is given.

chew on. It is literally like eating your food too fast and not being able to truly enjoy it. Too many times, I have witnessed people who were so anxious to get their prophetic word out that as soon as one person stops speaking, they immediately start speaking what they want to say. Several things can happen. The message may not be in the flow of what the Lord is doing, or it can be very overwhelming to the recipient. The recipient may completely forget what was said previously. It is similar to eating your food too fast. When you do that, you miss out on the enjoyment of the various flavors. Some fast eaters do not remember what they ate. It can be the same in prophetic ministry when too much information is relayed too quickly.

> Luke 10:1 *Now after this the Lord appointed seventy others, and sent them in pairs ahead of Him to every city and place where He Himself was going to come.*

Take your time to listen to what the Lord is saying through the other members of the team. Discern with the Holy Spirit, and you will be surprised by how consistent the message will be. Each message ties in with a previous message. One word will build upon the other. When it is done correctly, it is a beautiful thing, and many people can be blessed.

> Mat 18:16 *"But if he does not listen to you, take one or two more with you, so that BY THE MOUTH OF TWO OR THREE WITNESSES EVERY FACT MAY BE CONFIRMED."*

We can see clearly from the scripture above one advantage of ministry with a partner is accountability and confirmation. It is always good to have a witness present when you are doing ministry. People hear through many different types of filters. It is not unusual for you to be ministering and saying one thing and something completely different is heard by the person being ministered to. When you have a witness present, it can definitely clear up any confusion and give a measure of safety to your ministry.

The devil loves to twist our words. He loves to filter what we hear. When there is a witness present, if there is any question, the witness can definitely bring clarity to the situation.

1 Cor 13:9 *For we know in part and we prophesy in part;*

I do not think it is taking the above scripture out of context to say that no one has the whole picture. When we prophesy, it is not the entire message of God, obviously. When we minister, what we do and say is never perfect. But one beautiful thing about having a team is that each one can prophesy a part of the message. It is not unusual to have one person literally complete the thought of the person before him. The Lord may be telling a story to the person being ministered to, each minister can have a part of the story to tell. It is really amazing when this happens, and it is actually not uncommon at all

CHAPTER 17, TRUST AND OBEY

1.   When we walk with the Lord in the light of His
Word,
What a glory He sheds on our way!
While we do His good will, He abides with us still,
And with all who will trust and obey.

o   *Refrain:*
Trust and obey, for there's no other way
To be happy in Jesus, but to trust and obey.

2.   Not a shadow can rise, not a cloud in the skies,
But His smile quickly drives it away;
Not a doubt or a fear, not a sigh or a tear,
Can abide while we trust and obey.

3.   Not a burden we bear, not a sorrow we share,
But our toil He doth richly repay;
Not a grief or a loss, not a frown or a cross,
But is blessed if we trust and obey.

4.   But we never can prove the delights of His love
Until all on the altar we lay;
For the favor He shows, for the joy He bestows,
Are for them who will trust and obey.

5.   Then in fellowship sweet we will sit at His feet,
Or we'll walk by His side in the way;
What He says we will do, where He sends we will go;
Never fear, only trust and obey.

John H. Sammis, 1887

Trust and Obey, there is no other way. What a fantastic truth. That old hymn is over 130 years old but still speaks to us today. We have all heard what we must do is trust God. That is true. Trust is the equivalent of faith. We know that we are justified by faith, we are saved by faith, we are redeemed by faith, and we are made righteous by faith. We also know without faith, you cannot

Without faith you cannot please God

please God. Trusting God and believing in God is the fundamental truth of Christianity. However, God's word is clear that God wants us to do something more than simply trust him. Yes, trusting Him is preeminent. God tells us in His word that our faith or our trust without works is dead. In other words, it is essential to trust God and believe God, but it is just as important to obey God. You may say that trust is obedience, but if I am actually trusting God, then I am following Him and acting on His instructions.

James 2:17 *Even so faith, if it has no works, is dead, being by itself.*

In many charismatic churches today, the gift of prophecy is widespread. There is a part of the service where someone may come forward and be given a microphone. They will proceed to give a prophetic word to the church or to an individual. Sometimes near the end of the service, there will be an altar call, and people will come forward to receive ministry. Many times the people doing the ministry may speak prophetic words to individuals and the church. This gift is standard in many churches. But that is the problem. Because it is so common, I believe the gift has become undervalued. The first thing obviously is to determine if the prophetic word actually is a message from God. We have spoken previously in this book about many ways to determine if a word is from God or not. To determine if a message is from God have a thorough knowledge of the Bible. God will never contradict the Bible.

But because the gift has become common, I think the gift has become taken for granted. Many people who receive prophetic words will say something like thank you very much. I appreciate it. That really speaks to me, or that really encourages me. Sadly, after that so many times, the prophetic word is simply forgotten about. If God has given a message to an individual, there must be a response. The message may have a condition to it. The message may require faith. The message may require obedience. If God has spoken, then we need to pay meticulous attention to what was said and give an appropriate response.

I wrote earlier about the story of King Jehoshaphat and the three nations that came to destroy Judah. A prophetic word was given. The king and the people followed the instructions given in the prophecy, and the country was saved. That is a compelling lesson.

God is trying to give us answers that will save us from harm. He speaks to us the truth that will set us free. The Lord speaks words to us that demonstrate His love. He speaks to us answers to problems that seem to be unsolvable.

Often when God speaks, He is giving us specific instructions concerning how to overcome the situation that is plaguing us. Christians continually pray and ask God to deliver them and help them. God answers our prayers many times with a plan for success. But we fail to hear and then fail to act. I believe many of us are waiting for God to do something when God is waiting for us to follow the instructions that He gave us the last time He spoke to us.

> God gives specific instructions about how to overcome.

Sometimes God warns us with a feeling within our hearts. It is a feeling that something is not right, or we should not go that way. I have learned the hard way to pay attention to those feelings. Pay attention to that gut feeling that something is wrong.

God is very practical. The way He speaks to us is as a loving Father who wants to see us succeed. He is giving us steps to success if we will listen and take the steps. Perhaps you're looking for a job. God will tell you which company to send your resume to. Maybe you are struggling with what words to speak to your teenage son or daughter. God can talk to you and tell you exactly what to say to them and open up their heart. Maybe you are looking for an answer to the struggles in your marriage. God can give you a specific plan to follow that can bring healing to your marriage if you follow it by hearing God's voice and responding. All of this comes if we listen and take the next step, which is obedience.

A few years ago, I was troubled about something my wife was doing that was bothering me. When I prayed, I felt the Lord telling me not to say anything, be still, forgive her and love her, a change would come. I did precisely that, and change happened. Thank you Lord.

The primary point is we need to do more than simply ask God to help us, ask God to heal us, ask God to save us, and all those prayers that we typically pray. It is perfectly okay to petition God. But I think we have become entrenched in the habit of petitioning God and not listening to His voice when He speaks, and then if He does speak, we are not obeying him.

> We need to do more than ask God for help.

God is interested in everything in your life, He has solutions that will improve every aspect of your daily living. These solutions come from your ability to hear God's voice, trust God's voice, and obey

God's voice with your actions. If you follow this you will succeed God is never going to instruct you into failure.

Look at the last line that beautiful hymn *Trust and Obey* –

What He says we will do, where He sends we will go;
Never fear, only trust and obey.

Will you do what the Lord says? Will you go where the Lord sends you? Will you trust His voice and obey Him? You cannot do any of this unless you can hear God's voice. God is speaking to you. Right now, I believe the Lord is speaking to you. Can you hear Him?

God is speaking to you now.

If you hear Him, will you obey him? Do you understand that your obedience to God's voice is critical to the well-being of your family and your personal life?

The prophetic gift, when operating correctly, is God's voice. Remember, God can speak to you personally in your heart, and God can speak to you prophetically through other people. Regardless of how He speaks to you, the critical thing is to trust and obey.

CHAPTER 18, BEFORE YOU WERE BORN

Jeremiah 1:5 *"Before I formed you in the womb I knew you, And before you were born I consecrated you; I have appointed you a prophet to the nations."*

When you are born, some believe there was a conversation in heaven that went something like this- God speaking to Gabriel – "Well look Gabriel now we've got this baby named Ray. I am not sure what we will do with him. Let us just see how he develops, then we'll figure out something for him later."

As ridiculous as that sounds, that is the way many people live their life. They live a day to day existence trying to figure out what they want to do. They try to figure out how to be able to do what they want to do. They try to figure out what they want because their ideas have changed. Later they try to figure out how to get out of a dysfunctional relationship. Then they try to figure out how to get out of the job, which is boring them to tears. Later they try to figure out how they're going to make enough money to retire and live in a beachside resort and then finally just try to figure out what life really means. Finally, they realize that they have never been truly happy.

The hard truth is until you are doing what you were created to do in the place you were created to do it, you will never be completely satisfied. You will be in a constant state of searching for fulfillment. Unfortunately, many people look for substitutes for an unfulfilled life.

People look for substitutes for an unfulfilled like

The substitutes which actually never work are things like money, fame, or position. Or they can be destructive like alcohol, drugs, overeating, sexual addiction, depression, and other life-controlling substitutes.

Until you are satisfied with your life, you will never escape the trap of never enough. Money is never enough. Worldly success is never enough. Appearance is never enough. Having a high position is never enough. Material things are never enough (including your man toys). None of these things are enough to bring you satisfaction and fulfillment.

The only thing that will bring you happiness and fulfillment is your relationship with God, the presence of the Holy Spirit within you, and living a life in alignment with the purpose you were created for.

But what is that purpose? How do you know for sure what it is? If I find my purpose, how can I make the changes to get into it? Your purpose is not a great mystery. However, with that said, I honestly believe that Satan tries to obscure and hide your purpose by continually tempting you in wrong directions. It is a sad truth, but the Devil has a strategy. His strategy is always to come between God's people and God's plans. His schemes are accomplished by various methods. The most common practice is a temptation, which is a doorway to sin. His other devices include worldly desires, lousy teaching and influence, unhealthy relationships and other various evil schemes.

As I have said before, Satan cannot defeat God directly. He attacks God indirectly. He attacks God's people not to destroy the people but to destroy God's plan working through the people. He will fail because you have the Spirit of God within you. The power of the Holy Spirit is much greater than any scheme of the devil. We must find God's plan for our life and get into it. God is very interested, and He is always available to help you find your purpose.

> The Holy Spirit is greater than any scheme of Satan.

I was having a conversation with my wife just the other day talking about our son when he went to college and failed to finish his degree. She said he could not get into the major he wanted, so he just quit. She said he was struggling trying to determine what he wanted to do. With all respect and love for my beautiful wife, I told her that was a problem in his past. Most of the time, what young people want to do and desire to do is not what God has called them to do. Since that time, our son joined the Air Force, and it has fit him like a glove. He has succeeded in many ways, and I am very proud of him.

I am at a place in my life when I hate to hear the phrase, "What do you want to do?" I am not trying to be overly harsh because individual desires are important. But I also know that our desires can get us into a lot of trouble. I have been a victim of my own desires many times. I am actually an expert at following my personal passion and suffering the consequences. It is not a question of wanting to do something, it is a question of being designed to do something. The beauty of this is when you find your design, you will also find the appropriate desire for that design. But until you discover your created design, your wishes can lead you into all kinds of wrong directions. In the long run, the consequence is going to be a delay in finding your ultimate peace.

> I have been a victim of my own desires.

In my life, I know that I was called to be a minister of the Gospel of Jesus Christ at a young age. I had all kinds of desires throughout my life. I desired to be a rock and roll musician. I wanted to be wealthy through entrepreneurship. I desired to be a full-time writer living on a sailboat traveling the world. There was nothing inherently wrong with my desires except that my desires cost me about a 20-year delay in finding the reason I was born.

As I spoke about in earlier chapters in this book, let me emphasize how God is trying to let you know what He created you to do. In your life, there are moments when you are in a particular place doing a specific thing, and everything seems to fall in line with a supernatural peace that feels incredibly natural and wonderfully alive. I believe these moments are clear evidence of your creative design. It may not be exactly what you are doing, but it is a picture of what you are called to do.

Remember a time in my life when I was a businessman. I was working for a large company, and I was asked to give a presentation at a business conference. I thought and thought about the presentation and prepared very hard for it. I got up to speak in front of a room full of businessmen and their wives at a beautiful hotel conference center. I was nervous, but I walked out on stage and gave a presentation. I added a lot of humor to it, and the audience roared. It made a massive impact on me. That was about 35 years ago, and I remember it like it was yesterday. Now I realize I was not created to be a secular businessman, but the ability to get up and speak to people in a meaningful way was part of my created purpose. I was selling worldly goods at that time, but I have often said my real call is to sell the Gospel of Jesus Christ to anyone who will hear.

God was trying to show me something. When you do what you were created to do, it just works. If you have ever used a socket wrench, you know you have to find the correct socket, or you will have difficulty in completing the job. But when you find the socket that fits perfectly, it is no problem to tighten or loosen any bolt. You are the perfect socket to complete the job you were born to do.

What moments in your past gave you peace?

Look back at your life. What moments made you feel at peace? What were the moments when you felt most alive? What were you doing at that time? What seems to always come naturally to you? What were you doing in your past that always helped and served other people? These are clues to help you discover your purpose.

Sometimes it takes outside help to figure out what God wants you to do. If it were not for friends and family reminding me of things that I do well, I would have missed a lot of God's clues. Interestingly, your real friends and family often see more in you than you do and yourself. Other people who love you can be more objective about your talents and skills then our own over-analytical and critical selves.

You may be at the point where you know you have been going in the wrong direction or perhaps just a little bit off course. You feel something is not quite right, and you have never been totally content. I want you to know that God understands this, and God loves to give us another chance if we will simply repent, ask for His forgiveness, and ask Him to help. God wants us to be in the right place, doing the right thing. I call it your promised land, and it is a great place to be. It is a place of blessing to you and a blessing to others. God will help you make the change in your life to get there. You need to seek Him with all your heart and ask for His help. He will open up doors for you to move you to where He desires you to be and help you to do what he needs you to do.

Psalms 37:23 *The steps of a man are established by the LORD, And He delights in his way.*

God loves to establish our steps. He loves to show us a step to take and then wait to see if we take it before He shows us the next one. The good news for you is that you can find your way just by taking one step at a time. God loves this method because it involves more faith and trust. Ask God to help you. Ask God to show you the next step and take it. I promise you when you take the next step, the following steps will become clear. When you take Step 2, the Lord will show you step 3. That is the way God works. Our nature is to want to see the next 27 steps before we take the first one. That is not going to work with God, So relax and trust Him. Take just one step and watch what happens. You are going to love it!

CHAPTER 19, HOW TO AVOID BEING WEIRD

I consider myself to be, in most ways, just a regular guy. I love to do the things that guys do, and I think the way that guys think, I was raised in a middle-class home in Memphis, Tennessee. I attended a neighborhood elementary school, then junior high and high school. I went to college, got a job, and got married. I define myself as a normal American man. I know that everyone is different, but there are some similarities with a lot of guys. I love sports. I love college football, NFL football, NBA basketball, college basketball, PGA Tour golf. You get the idea. For hobbies, I love sailing, fishing, gardening, and golf. I have a wife and four grown children and four grandchildren.

I think I am a typical American male. I am not going to underemphasize that because being an average American male is actually a great blessing. I have traveled to several countries, and one consistent thing is that when I get back to America, I always have a greater appreciation for our beautiful land.

In the context of being a supposedly normal person, if you interact with most people in our society and tell them that God speaks to you, they will think you are completely weird. You will probably be laughed at. Or perhaps they will just whisper under their breath, roll their eyes a little bit, and walk away. They may think you are a member of a cult or delusional. Or you cannot be serious.

Find people who can support your walk with God.

However, I am very blessed to have a broad group of friends who do hear the voice of God and have a real appreciation for anyone else who does the same. You must find people in your life who can support your walk with God. As for me, there is only one spiritual view that is correct. It is the view that Jesus Christ is the Son of God who came to save the world for anyone who would believe in Him. He is the way, the truth and the life and no one comes to the Father but through Him (John 14:6). I am not going into an apologetic argument here about Christ. However, anyone who will research the truth with an objective mind will come to a scientific, legal, and historical view that Christianity is the truth. When someone believes that there are many ways to God, it offends me because that is making Jesus Christ a liar. When they say they can believe in Jesus and also other ways again, they have no idea who Jesus is.

With that being said, it is crucial to find a church that understands and teaches the Bible. This church needs to also know that the author of the Bible is very much alive and still speaking to us. That is what the Bible teaches. If the Bible teaches this, we should experience it. Again, it is unfortunate that some Christians believe the only way God ever speaks is through the Bible when the Bible itself teaches that God speaks to us in many ways. I have actually never understood that logic. Generally speaking, in the Christian realm, there are two types of churches. There are traditional churches and what is known as Spirit-filled churches. The conventional churches believe the gifts of the Spirit, including things such as prophecy, have all ceased. The Spirit-filled churches believe the gifts of the Spirit are still in existence and God is speaking to us in many ways today. To me, it is a no-brainer as to which group I would rather be part of. I do not mean this to be offensive to my other brothers and sisters in Christ. I just know what the Bible says, and I also know what I have experienced in my relationship with the Lord.

So how do I keep from being weird? I know some very weird Christians. These are the ones that might sit in a public restaurant and began speaking in tongues and prophesying to everyone around them. They may walk up to strangers and say, "God is giving me a prophetic word for you. Can I lay my hands on you and heal you?" I am not trying to ridicule them, but I know that many times unintentionally, they come across as being strange and can actually do damage to the reputation of Christ.

Of course, Jesus was very different. Some people may have thought He was weird. Most people at that time felt that He was a radical and a heretic. This did not stop Jesus from doing the will of His Father. Jesus had amazing courage and boldness when He walked the earth. I have learned in my walk with the Lord that the Holy Spirit can give me boldness and courage when I least expect it. It may seem weird to some people, but actually, you are just doing what God has directed you to do.

> The Holy Spirit can give you boldness when you least expect it.

I have given prophetic words to servers at restaurants and customers in department stores. I prayed for strangers and have seen them healed. At the same time, I do not think I was coming across as a crazy person. Acting foolish does no benefit to the kingdom of God. The obvious question is, how do you balance being bold and courageous for Christ and not seeming insane?

To me, the answer is love and compassion. When a person knows that you genuinely care about them and have compassion for them, they become very open to whatever you have for them. Just in living day-to-day, I have countless times run across strangers and immediately felt a level of Christian love and compassion for them. So many times, I had no idea why I was feeling the way that I felt. It may be someone that I just had a conversation with at a store or neighbor that I meet walking down the sidewalk. Sometimes I would just get this profound feeling inside that there was something more to this chance meeting. When these meetings come it is important to handle it appropriately. If you handle it correctly, you will not be considered weird.

A few weeks ago, I was at the gym. In this gym, there are two swimming pools. One is a lap pool. The other is known as a therapeutic pool. I swam a few laps and came very close to breaking Michael Phelps Olympic record in freestyle and the butterfly (perhaps a slight exaggeration). After my Olympic records, I proceeded to the therapeutic pool. In this pool, there was a lady who was walking around through the water very slowly. Somehow, we started talking, and she began to share with me that she was an 8th-grade teacher who had fallen and hurt her knee very badly. She was concerned that she was not going to be able to do her job. The school was getting ready to start, and she did not know if she was going to be able to handle the classroom situation. At this point, I could have become weird and said: "do you mind if I lay hands and pray for your healing and give you a prophetic word?" That probably would have done more damage than good. As we conversed, she asked me what I did for a career. I told her was I was a former pastor. As we talked, she opened up that she was a Christian too. I was able to share with her some of the supernatural things I have seen as a pastor. I also was able to share with her how God can supernaturally heal her knee. The Holy Spirit was speaking to me as I was talking to her, and he seemed to be guiding my words. I did not say anything that would "freak her out." I was able to speak in a way that she could easily digest, and I really think before she left the pool that day, she knew that God had touched her.

> The Holy Spirit spoke to me as I talked to her.

Sometimes when I encounter people, and I know that God is giving me a prophetic word for them. I just simply say, "Hello, what's your name?" Then I will say, "My name is Ray. I am a pastor, and I feel like when I met you that the Lord wanted me to tell you something. Is that okay?" 99.9% of the time people will tell you, "Sure." Then I will say what I am sensing the Lord wants me to speak to the person. Sometimes it is concrete and detailed. Other times it is very general. But I do not come across as weird or strange, and what I am saying is quickly received.

I am not ashamed of my faith. I am not ashamed that God speaks to me, and He lets me talk for Him many times. I know many people think it is strange and non-traditional. I will not ever knowingly disown my savior, but I do want to represent Him in a way that can be received without compromising my faith. I guess you could say it is a fine line between acting weird or hiding who you really are. I think it is essential to be able to present the truth of Christ in a way that people can receive without compromising the truth of Christ.

> I am not ashamed that God speaks to me and allows me to speak to others for Him

If you allow the Holy Spirit to lead you and literally asked him to put his words in your mouth, you will be able to say the exact words that people need to hear in a way that they can understand and receive. This is very critical. Do not jump ahead of God. I have witnessed some Christians try to force the issue instead of being patient and letting God give them the correct timing and the right words. When you allow the Holy Spirit to do this, you will never come across as weird. You will come across as someone who genuinely cares for other people. That is a message that everyone can understand and appreciate.

I love hearing God's voice and the power of the Holy Spirit. I love flowing in the gifts of the Holy Spirit. I love the supernatural power of God. When I read the Bible, that is what I see all over the New Testament. God is alive and well and wanting to move in our midst. It is sad that in our society and culture, we have reduced Him to more of a story in history instead realizing He is alive and is offering us spiritual power, full of love, joy, and peace. God is a real person who desires an intimate relationship with us.

CHAPTER 20, YES, YOU CAN HAVE IT BOTH WAYS!

Well, they say you cannot have it both ways. At least that is what my mama told me. Actually, with the Holy Spirit and God, you can have it both ways. Some things are true, regardless of what one may believe. The Earth is round. The Sun is hot. Gravity really works. The Miami Dolphins are a terrible football team. (Sorry just had to throw that in.) We live in a natural world, and we live in a spiritual world. That is reality, and it is not a question of belief. It is a simple truth.

Many people believe they are only living entirely in the natural world their entire life. That is partly true. We are living in a natural world. They have their natural senses operating. (Of course, some people live in nonsense). The natural realm is normal. It can be seen tasted, felt, and touched. There is comfort about the natural realm because it

> Unfortunately, many people believe the natural world is all there is.

is understandable. We, humans, love things we can understand and control. I spoke about that earlier in this book. We love to be in control. It is normal and natural for us. However, it is not God's plan for us, and it is not God's best for us. Living in the natural realm brings a sense of security. However, it was actually false security. In the natural realm, we follow our desires. In the natural realm, we follow our plans. In the natural, you mostly know what to expect even though you are continually being hit with the unexpected. The natural realm is comfortable because it is incredibly familiar. The natural realm is so commonplace that many people have a complete unawareness of anything beyond their natural senses.

1 Cor 2:14 *But a natural man does not accept the things of the Spirit of God, for they are foolishness to him; and he cannot understand them, because they are spiritually appraised.*

The problem or the reality is that while we are living in the natural realm, there is a spiritual realm that is having a tremendous influence on us. When we are born again and receive the Holy Spirit, an immense change takes place in us. We have brand new abilities that we did not have before. One of these fundamental abilities is to understand the things of God and the spiritual realm in which we are living in twenty-four hours a day. 1 Cor 2:12 Now *we have received, not the spirit of the world, but the Spirit who is from God, so that we may know the things freely given to us by God,*

The natural realm and the spiritual realm operate simultaneously. Some people are aware of it some people are not. It is foolish to be unaware of the spiritual realm because it is having a powerful impact on your natural world. Believe it or not. Just like the sun will rise in the east, whether you believe it or not, there is a spiritual realm that is influencing your life tremendously.

> **The natural realm and the spiritual realm exist simultaneously.**

In the spiritual realm, there is the Holy Spirit of God. The Holy Spirit brings glory and credit to Jesus Christ. There are also other spirits in the spiritual realm, which are there for your harm. These are demon spirits, and they have one job, and that job is to steal, kill, and rob you.

John 10:10" The *thief comes only to steal and kill and destroy. But the spirit that belongs to Jesus Christ that is the holy spirit has another job and it is I came that they may have life, and have it abundantly.*"

So why would you not want to be completely aware? The natural realm is reasonable, comfortable, and kind of thoughtless. But there is a spiritual realm which can do two things, the spiritual realm can bring you life and life more abundantly, or the spiritual realm can steal from you rob you and even kill you.

In the spiritual realm, we have been given authority over evil spirits. But authority is useless unless it is operated. So, the situation we are living in is this. We can live a natural life unaware of the spiritual realm, and we will be influenced in potentially very harmful ways by that spiritual world. When we are aware of the spiritual realm, we know, and we have power over anything that would hurt us. The result is we are left with the favor and blessings of God.

There is a war going on in the spirit realm between the Holy Spirit and demon spirits. The Holy Spirit is in control, but the demon spirits can be given right away and legal means to harm us through our ignorance.

> **There is a war between the Holy Spirit and demon spirits.**

When we know the Lord, we have to know Him spiritually because God is a spirit. To know the Holy Spirit is to know Jesus and God. The Bible explains this very clearly in this verse:

John 16:14 – 15" He *will glorify Me, for He will take of Mine and will disclose it to you. All things that the Father has are Mine; therefore, I said that He takes of Mine and will disclose it to you.*"

In the above verse, Jesus is referring to the Holy Spirit. God gives to Jesus. Jesus gives to the Holy Spirit, and the Holy Spirit gives to us. It is the Holy Spirit who gives us revelation knowledge of God.

In the Christian life to be able to be fully appreciative of the natural world which God has created is fantastic. To be aware of the spiritual world, which God has created, is vital. When you have an awareness of both realms, you are living life to the fullest. Jesus wants us to have life abundantly. To have that, we have to be aware of both realms.

To me, the spirit realm ads spice to life. The spirit realm is the icing on the cake and another level of living. Being in the natural and the spiritual simultaneously is a blessed way to live!

In this book, I have written about hearing God's voice. My desire is for you to be able to hear the voice of God speaking to you, giving you instructions for your life. I want you to hear God speaking to you, telling you how to overcome. I want you to hear God speaking to you, showing you how to be a blessing to those around you. I want you to hear God speaking to you so you can be healed and completely free of any bondage or heartbreak. I want you to hear God's voice so you can be a better husband or a better wife. I want you to hear God's voice so you can be a better parent.

I want you to hear God's voice so you can express God's desire and God's will for those who have been assigned to you. This includes your friends, your family, your community, and your church. When I use the expression "be God's voice," I don't want you to be prideful. I want you to be humble and learn how to follow God's instructions and leading and speak what He tells you to speak and act when He tells you to move and do what He tells you to do. That is what it means to be God's voice. It means to be a witness for Christ. It means to be a better leader. It means to be able to impact people for the kingdom of God and bring truth and healing and love to this world that is

> Hear God's voice so you can express God's will for those who have been assigned to you.

suffering so much. Being God's voice is a major part fulfilling your purpose and call. Being God's voice is laying hands on the sick and believing for their healing. Being God's voice is being bold and sharing with others with the Lord has done for you. Being God's voice allows you to be a wise counselor, a better minister, and overall, just a better person.

I pray that this book has been helpful to you. Hear His voice and be His cry is something all Christians are called to do. I hope this book taught you and encouraged you. I hope this book is something that you would love to share with others. I pray God's blessing and favor and anointing and power and love on all those who read this book.

Hearing Gods voice can be the most important thing you will ever do in your life.

Please feel free to check out my website at www.icmcollege.org. On this site, you will find some valuable free college lessons and other offers. If you desire to complete your education with a Holy Spirit-filled seminary on our web site, we offer a free evaluation so you will know what the requirements would be for your college degree. If you believe that you are called into the ministry, the International College of Ministry is a great place to get your training. It is entirely online, and you work on your own schedule. Most of our students will complete their degree in 12 months. It is accredited and affordable with no interest payment plans. I would love to hear from you! You can email me at drray@icmcollege.org

Blessings – Dr. Ray Self

Beloved, I pray that in all respects you may prosper and be in good health, just as your soul prospers.
3 John 1:2